8/16

Victim Zero

KAT WARD

Victim Zero

Jimmy Savile tried to ruin my life.
I was the first victim to fight back.

JOHN BLAKE

Published by John Blake Publishing Limited,
3 Bramber Court, 2 Bramber Road,
London W14 9PB, England

www.johnblakepublishing.co.uk

www.facebook.com/johnblakebooks
twitter.com/jblakebooks

First published in paperback in 2016

ISBN: 978-1-78606-029-7

British Library Cataloguing-in-Publication Data:
A catalogue record for this book is available from the British Library.

Design by www.envydesign.co.uk

Printed in Great Britain by CPI Group (UK) Ltd

1 3 5 7 9 10 8 6 4 2

Papers used by John Blake Publishing are natural, recyclable products made
from wood grown in sustainable forests. The manufacturing processes conform
to the environmental regulations of the country of origin.

Every attempt has been made to contact the relevant copyright-holders, but
some were unobtainable. We would be grateful if the appropriate people could
contact us.

Victim: *noun*: 'Someone who has been hurt or killed.'
Zero: *adjective*: 'Not any or none.'

This book is dedicated to all victims
without a voice.

Contents

Chapter One

Location: David Price Solicitors & Advocates, Fleet Street,
London, and Royal Courts of Justice, Strand, London

Timeline: 15 June 2015 – day one of the case

sue: *verb*: 'To take legal action against a person or organisation,
especially by making a legal claim for money because of some
harm that they have caused you.'

I'd hardly slept a wink the previous night, and the journey
to my solicitor's office in a fancy black Mercedes (when
we'd merely asked the hotel to order a taxi to convey us) didn't
help one bit: by the time the vehicle pulled up outside the office
I felt thoroughly sick as well as tired. Peter (of whom more
later) and I were warmly welcomed by Stuart, who invited us
to sit and wait in the reception area while Helen and Yinka
gathered the remaining bits and pieces. I sat beside Peter and
watched as Yinka struggled with several heavy-looking boxes
balanced on a trolley. Helen emerged from somewhere behind
the reception area and offered me the scarf she'd said she could
lend me; none of my clothing entirely covered my tattoos and
Helen had advised me to try and obscure them all if possible.

When I'd arranged the scarf around my neck to successfully

hide the skin-art that might cause me to be judged solely on appearance, Helen advised me that there would probably be an assortment of press people loitering outside the court. My face must have given away my feelings of dread because she then smiled and added that we shouldn't let that worry us as she possessed 'extremely sharp elbows'. I had a fleeting mental image of my diminutive solicitor felling journalists and photographers alike, but before I could laugh properly, David Price came to greet us.

Although I'd spoken to everyone from the solicitor's practice on multiple occasions, I'd only ever met David in person just once, on the day he agreed to take on my case. Then, he'd been wearing casual trousers and a tatty old sweater. On that Monday morning, he looked immaculate in his QC's uniform; not only that, he radiated both confidence and competence.

My feelings, aside from the physical weariness and nausea due to lack of sleep, had been mixed, right up until the moment I saw David ready to run the gauntlet on my behalf. I cannot claim I'd been frightened, as such; that would be entirely the wrong descriptor for the emotions roiling within. I'd felt resigned and hugely irritated by the whole 'being sued' business. And obviously, I'd been experiencing high levels of anxiety (although probably not in the way most people might have imagined) in the weeks leading up to this day, the beginning of a case which should never, ever have been permitted to come to court in the first place. Mainly, I'd felt angry, far angrier than I'd ever been in my life. However, that anger began to evolve and mutate into something more positive as I listened to David explain how things would proceed once we were in court; a trickle of belief, or perhaps confidence, began to shape and hone my anger into a far more useful emotion: righteous anger. Suddenly, the nausea vanished and I sat up a little straighter. It no longer mattered to me that I'd been utterly abandoned by those who had hounded me for the information and then, having profited from the scandalous revelations, callously walked away, leaving me to fight this immense battle alone. It didn't matter any more. No, what mattered now was that I hold my ground. I'd done nothing wrong, after all.

Helen opened the office door and together we stepped out onto Fleet Street, already sizzling in the midsummer heat at nine-thirty in the morning. I sniffed the air and noted that smell, peculiar to London, so difficult to describe but as familiar and comforting as it was unpleasant. The scarf instantly stuck to my neck and I became uncomfortably aware, as we walked in a group towards the court, that I had begun to perspire profusely.

I leaned on my cane with one hand and wished I could grab at Peter with the other as we approached the rather beautiful Gothic-looking building from across the road. 'The Royal Courts of Justice' in black iron-wrought words stood out, almost three-dimensionally to my eyes, against the pale stone architecture, and caught my attention.

As Peter escorted me alongside the building with Helen on my other side, I silently pondered the word 'justice'. I had managed to survive into adulthood (after a fashion) with a strong personal sense of justice, although I realised, as we slipped past a couple of press photographers unnoticed, that

I'd never really experienced, or even expected, any kind of justice to be applied to me. The tip of my cane slid on the well-trodden stone and I stumbled a little as we went up the steps and through the doors.

I'd been forewarned, of course, by my legal team, that I'd be required to face 'airport-style' security but, since I've never been abroad or travelled by air, the warning meant little to me. I dumped my handbag and cane into the basket supplied and informed the fellow watching them pass through the scanner that I was carrying scissors within my stoma supplies. He nodded acknowledgement and then I walked through the scanning archway, mildly surprised that the alarm had not sounded because my stoma bag is fastened with (of all things) a small metal fold-back paper clip. I did have to show the stoma supplies and the tiny curved scissors within the pack but, apparently, these did not present any kind of threat and I was free to continue to the court.

The opponent, and the sole reason for my having to attend at the Royal Courts of Justice some two hundred miles from my home, was already in the courtroom, along with a large crowd of people, all of whom were clearly 'his side'. There he was: One Famous Person, seated in a wheelchair and wearing some kind of oxygen mask, huffing and puffing as his personal nurse fussed with medication and inhalers. I tried not to goggle, because he was the epitome of a frail, sick and elderly man, not at all like the foul-mouthed, enraged entertainer who had, just three and a half years previously, ranted and raged on stage to a live audience about me and had denounced everything

I'd said as lies. Anyone would think this pathetic figure was the defendant, not the arrogant, furious Claimant Surely, I thought, this poor fellow couldn't really expect to still be giving live shows to a paying audience? And then, it dawned on me: of course not. And in his view, the reason he could not do so any more was absolutely and entirely my fault; I'd done this to him, in his opinion. I wondered, briefly, whether he also held me responsible for his fourth wife having recently left him. Probably, was the only conclusion I could come to.

I sat on the front bench, next to Helen, my solicitor, on my right and Peter on my left; before us, on the narrow oak table, several crammed lever-arch files barely left room for the carafe of water and three glasses. David Price stood behind and when I turned, briefly, to glance at him, I noticed he had similar files and also a set of impressive leather-bound tomes on the table before him. I studied the courtroom overtly, paying particular attention to the plentiful woodwork: rich-toned, well-aged and meticulously polished oak. Several trees must have been sacrificed in order to make the seating, panelling, tables and window frames. I experienced a weird sensation… as if time itself had been captured and pinned down like a special butterfly, a disembodied presence observing the proceedings with utter indifference. This felt odd, but not frightening.

Forcing my mind to focus on what was happening and how I came to be sitting in this imposing room waiting for the judge to enter turned out to be difficult; my brain simply did not want to deal with it in any meaningful way, although I felt no fear, or even awe. Perhaps this in itself meant there might be something fundamentally wrong with me, I thought. Surely, I was supposed to feel frightened and cowed? Shouldn't I be sitting, quivering with unsuppressed panic, expecting the world to fall in on me? After all, it's not every day a Famous Person summons one to court in order to sue for special damages in the sum of three hundred thousand pounds. All this kerfuffle, over a few words I'd written in my personal memoirs, which I started publishing online from 2009, and repeated, in interview, to two journalists. Perhaps my fearlessness came down to the simple fact that I'd never had three hundred thousand pounds, nor was I ever in any way likely to have that kind of money, and besides, what I'd said was true.

Mr Dean Dunham, evidently the leader of the Claimant's team, had, in the run-up to the actual court case, made much of my age at the time of the incident of which I had spoken, claiming that I'd been over the age of sixteen when it happened. I'd been completely befuddled by this because, in my view, it wouldn't have mattered a jot whether I'd been a fifteen-year-old schoolgirl, a young mother in my mid-twenties or a divorcee and mother of many in my thirties. The Claimant had said something so cruel to me that it would have caused the same emotional and psychological injuries whatever my age. Never having had much in the way of self-esteem or confidence, what little I possessed or pretended to possess had always been easily tattered and damaged, sometimes completely destroyed.

In my opinion, the Claimant hadn't done anything wrong in particular, only acted in exactly the same way as every young fellow (and plenty of older fellows too) did towards women of all ages during the early seventies. He'd jokingly begun to 'goose' me – that is, to grab at the underside of my buttocks over my clothing and say the word 'goose'. Then when I jumped (making a movement which tucked the buttocks away from his hand, itself making the chest thrust forward, which was the usual response), he had grabbed a handful of out-thrust breast and said 'honk, honk'. This was supposed to be funny – but he smelled uncannily like my stepfather and that reminded me of many horrors, so I'd recoiled, instantly hysterical as I attempted to get out of his reach, trying to escape, waving my arms about like a demented windmill whilst crying out, 'Don't touch me!' This was not at all the way women (of any age) were supposed to react to such things and must have been acutely embarrassing for him. Being a comedian and quick-witted, not to mention observant, he'd remarked, 'I wouldn't want to touch you anyway; you're a titless wonder!' Everyone roared with laughter, of course, and I burned with shame and humiliation whilst wishing fervently that the floor would open up and swallow me.

Unfortunately for me, what he'd said was true: I'd not been blessed with breasts like every other girl my age and my lack of womanly curves caused me no end of anguished envy on a daily basis. Being tall and extremely slender only accentuated my missing attributes and it helped not one bit that the clothes I wore could only charitably be called 'old-fashioned'. In fact, my wardrobe contents had always been absolutely dreadful. I may well have been resident and in the care of a 'Home Office Approved School for Intelligent but Emotionally Disturbed

Girls', but Mother still provided the things I had to wear and her choices had been distinctly strange and outdated all my life long. Adolescent girls are not the most pleasant of creatures at the best of times and I'd grown well used to the teasing, taunting and torment relating to my attire. Now, the delightful guest of Sir Jimmy Savile OBE (who was evidently charmed by at least one of the other Duncroft schoolgirls) had, albeit unwittingly, given my peers another, more powerful weapon with which to hurt me. Being flat-chested was bad enough, but to have it remarked upon by a male celebrity in front of forty or more people was unbearable, and I knew, instinctively, the other girls would never let me forget the incident even for a moment.

Actually, the remark stung for many, many years and certainly had a hand in my complete inability to hold any kind of meaningful relationship together. I'd never become secure enough within myself to believe that anybody wanted me for myself, just as I was. Whenever I'd noticed a boyfriend or husband even glancing at a woman with ample bosoms, I would feel immediately inadequate, worthless and less than a proper woman. I'd shout, physically attack or make wild accusations of planned or actual infidelity. Under a rain of blows or a stream of verbal abuse, even the most mild-mannered of men can only stand so much, particularly when half the time they'd not even been aware that their gaze had rested, however briefly, on another woman's figure.

I turned in my seat and watched as the Claimant had a coughing fit. I knew he was aware of my gaze, but he didn't acknowledge me in any way. I firmly believed that he hadn't the faintest clue how much more damage he was doing now, or even if he did, whether or not he cared. Why should he care about me? I thought as I watched both his legal team and his carer do what they could to help him to breathe. It was perfectly clear to me, right from the beginning, when my memory first became... public... that he neither remembered me nor the remark. For heaven's sake, he'd denied ever being at the BBC theatre at first.

Furthermore, he'd insisted that I'd 'picked his name out of a hat' and that he'd only ever met Sir Jimmy Savile, the National Treasure, a couple of times and had never been on any of his shows. When the footage of the show came to light, and everyone could see that not only had he been a guest on the show but that I had been seated right next to him, he said he'd been mistaken about that part and couldn't be expected to recall every show he'd ever done, but that what I'd said about our meeting was still absolutely untrue.

The Claimant had threatened to sue me if I didn't retract what I'd said about him to the Metropolitan Police investigation Operation Yewtree when they'd interviewed me about the Savile revelations. Or rather I'd taken two separate telephone calls from a woman claiming to be a journalist who told me of the Claimant's intention to take me to court unless I publicly apologised and stated also that what I'd said wasn't true. I'd actually laughed at her before I hung up, but the dart had flown true and I fretted and worried about the possibility of court proceedings. I absolutely couldn't retract what I'd said

9

because I'd told the truth as I remembered it. It had been such a dreadful occurrence and had hurt me so deeply that it had defined my self-image throughout my life. On the other hand, I couldn't afford to be sued. I had no assets: I didn't own my home and my car was more of a mobile shed and not worth more than about a hundred quid. I'd been alive for more than half a century and had nothing of material value to show for all those years. No antiques or jewellery, no furs or designer clothing for me; my bank balance was generally somewhere around 'zero' or in 'minus funds'.

Within a few days, the anxiety had got the better of me and I contacted the Metropolitan Police officer who had taken my statement and asked if it was possible for me to withdraw it. I wish I'd been told that if I withdrew my statement I'd leave the way clear for civil court action to be taken against me, but the police merely concentrated on the fact that I wasn't retracting what I'd said or changing it, just saying that I no longer wished to pursue the matter and so was withdrawing my statement. They actually asked if the Claimant had threatened me, but of course he hadn't, not directly. I did mention the alleged reporter but no one seemed to think what she'd said was in any way important.

When a woman's voice cut into my thoughts with 'All stand' I snapped back to the present and scrambled to my feet just before the judge entered the court. Everyone bowed their heads respectfully to him and so I did, too. The Claimant just sat in his wheelchair and scowled through his plastic oxygen mask. Helen leaned in close to me and whispered, 'I've never seen two people who wanted to be in court less than you and him.' It was true; I didn't want to be there at all for obvious reasons, and the Claimant's lawyers had tried, unsuccessfully, to have the case adjourned because their client was unwell with a 'serious lung complaint'. I'd had a fairly recent diagnosis of a lung condition myself; it may well even have been the same complaint (COPD – chronic obstructive pulmonary disorder), but I wouldn't have tried to use it as an excuse not to come to court.

The judge bowed to the court before he sat down and picked up a sheaf of papers. He looked, to my eyes, like a rather stern and certainly very proper gentleman and my heart sank a little. I fervently hoped that none of my tattoos were showing; the judge didn't look like a man who would approve of females with multiple – or indeed any – tattoos.

The case began, but my mind wandered again and I allowed myself to consider what might actually happen to me after the case had finished and I'd been found guilty of defamation, slander and libel and ordered to pay damages and costs… It never occurred to me there could be any other result because I believed that true justice didn't happen to people like me, not real justice, only the sort that superficially looks right – things like 'she has tattoos so she must therefore also drink too much alcohol and take illegal drugs and should be locked up,' and 'she's a single parent and a lazy scrounging good-for-nothing, so her brats will all be criminals and scroungers, too'. Over the years, I'd decided it was completely pointless to attempt to defend myself against such cruel generalisations and so I largely kept to myself and remained silent. I hoped that people would see for themselves, over time, that their suppositions were incorrect.

Of course, I knew some people wouldn't believe the evidence of their own eyes anyway and so I developed the view that, no matter how hard I tried, or whatever I did, I would be unpopular for the whole of my life and this couldn't ever be changed – just as Mother had drummed into me.

Chapter Two

mother: *noun*: 'A female parent.'
mother, to: *verb*: 'To treat a person with great kindness
and love and to try to protect them from anything
dangerous or difficult.'

Whenever I've asked other people what they recall of their very early childhood, the reply has been 'not much' or 'very little'. Now and again someone will relate one little snippet that has stayed with them, often something amusing, frightening or downright ridiculous. Right away, I'm aware that I'm different from other people because I can recall an awful lot, very vividly, of my childhood, from about the age of three. I'm also different because most of my childhood was frightening, miserable, painful, not to mention extremely lonely, and those memories flatly refuse to go away. I'm well into my sixth decade at the time of writing and even now, if I shut my eyes and think back, I can almost hear my mother's voice and the horrible things she said (or often screeched). Now and then, whilst going about my daily activities and encountering other people, occasionally a phrase might be uttered and I find myself emotionally hurled backward, some fifty-something years, to where the fear and pain are always waiting for me, ready to snatch me into a suffocating, terrifying and unwelcome embrace.

Mother didn't like me one bit and she never seemed to grow weary of telling me how dreadful I was. My vocabulary grew exponentially as ever more adjectives were hurled in my direction: disgusting; vile; scrawny; useless; stupid; revolting; selfish; greedy; worthless; ugly. I could go on and list a whole page of such negative words, but I think you'll get the picture from the few I've shared. The consequence of having all these negative words repeated, in a nasty tone of voice or shouted, was, unsurprisingly, a complete lack of self-esteem, which itself eventually made all the adjectives into truths via a kind of self-fulfilling-prophecy effect.

Nana – who had no children of her own and had adopted Mother from Barnardo's children's home at the age of three – treated me kindly and with infinite patience. My maternal grandmother was bemused when Mother told her the manner in which I allegedly behaved when at home with her in the little touring caravan where we lived, itself situated within the grounds of the hotel in Horning where Mother worked; Nana also lived in the village. They argued about me often because Nana couldn't accept many of the things Mother said about me when I was so little. Of course, I adored Nana; what child wouldn't adore the grandparent who showered them with affection, delighted in broadening their knowledge and awareness of the wide world, never stinted on paying close attention, and displayed nothing but pleasure and pride in every tiny achievement they made?

Unfortunately for me, Nana wasn't the only person who looked after me whilst Mother worked. Sometimes, one of Mother's friends, a woman I'll call 'Betty' although that's not her real name, would come and take me off to her cottage where I'd have to stay until Mother arrived to fetch me. Betty didn't like me much either. She scolded me often, slapped me frequently and threatened me all the time with the dire consequences I'd likely face when Mother came home. In fact, I didn't like Betty any more than she liked me, not that there was anything I could do about it; I certainly wouldn't have dared to say anything to Mother or even to Nana.

I'm pretty certain that my lifelong affliction of emetophobia (extreme fear of vomiting) began way back then, when I was just three years old and living with Mother in that horrible caravan. My 'room' was little more than a cupboard really, right at the back of the van. It comprised a small bunk built in atop a storage area beneath the tiny, grimy window and about eighteen inches of floor space. Mother locked me inside there every night; apparently, if she left the door unlocked, I would waste no time in making good my escape and creep out of the horrid, enclosed space to curl to sleep on the small settee in the living area, along with Matty, Mother's dog. Matty, a bearded collie with a gentle nature, only ever got into trouble when paying attention to me. Anyhow, I can remember, all too vividly, waking and being violently sick one night, all over myself, the little bed and my beloved 'lambie' – a knitted lamb

15

Nana had made for me – and the floor too. I was frightened to death because it was pitch dark in the little room, the stuff that had just erupted out of me stank to high heaven, I didn't understand what had happened in the least, my tummy hurt and I wanted my mummy, or my Nana or... I needed care and comfort and I cried out for it.

Of course, Mother was furious at being awoken. She had work to go to in the morning and saw my illness as a deliberate ploy to make her life even more difficult. She dragged my soiled nightwear off, getting vomit in my hair and my face – which caused me to retch loudly – snatched the soaked and reeking bedding away whilst demanding to know, at the top of her angry voice, how I thought she would have the time to deal with my filth. I cried, loudly, and stretched out my skinny little arms to her, pleading for comfort, but she tossed a plastic potty and a partially soiled blanket at me. She told me not to wake her again, threatened me with dire consequences if I did and then, switched off the light and left me. I heard her lock the door and bawled even more loudly. Mother shouted through the thin partition wall for me to shut up or she'd return and give me a hiding I'd not forget.

I was sick again, but I managed to get it into the potty, which almost overflowed. I didn't sleep much at all, but spent the night curled into the corner of my mattress, leaning against the wall clutching the edge of the blanket. Betty came to let me out in the morning and all she did was scold and nag; what a dirty, thoughtless little brat I was to have made such a dreadful mess when poor Mother had work to attend to.

Another powerful fear I had was of water... specifically, water submerging me or running over my head. If Nana ever needed to wash my hair, she would make me lie back in the bath whilst she gently washed and then rinsed my hair without ever getting any soap or water in my eyes or ears. Both Mother and Betty simply poured the (generally chilly) contents of the huge enamelled ewer over my head and then became furious with me when I thrashed about in utter panic, gasping and screaming whilst also making determined efforts to escape. I don't know what was worse: having sick caked into my straggly, tangled rat-tail-like hair or having a gallon of cold water poured over my head to rinse the foul stuff away, followed by being roughly scrubbed with coal tar soap. Lambie got soaked and scrubbed too, although Betty left him, hanging by one knitted ear, on a small line outside the caravan whilst we walked to her cottage. She wouldn't let me inside the house that day because she didn't want vomit on her furniture or carpets she said, so I sat on a groundsheet on the front lawn. It wasn't so bad; there wasn't much to do, but at least I didn't have to go inside where the place smelled strongly and most unpleasantly of 'old lady'. When Betty produced food I couldn't even look at it without retching, and this crime earned me a sound thrashing from Mother when she collected me after she finished work. Apparently, nice little girls didn't waste good food and I needed to be soundly spanked until I learned to be a nice little girl. Nobody would ever or could ever like me when I was so utterly revolting, selfish and hateful.

Chapter Three

Location: Court 13, Royal Courts of Justice,
Queen's Bench Division, Strand, London

Timeline: 15 June 2015 – day one of the case

helpless: *adjective*: 'Unable to do anything to help
yourself or anyone else.'

A section of the court – in fact, generally where a jury might have been seated – had been set aside for journalists because the case had been expected to garner a great deal of attention. In reality, there were only three reporters present: two men and a woman. From their seats they were able to observe the whole courtroom and were positioned extremely well to see both my own and the Claimant's faces. Of course, being in a wheelchair meant that the Claimant did not have to stand (or sit) in the witness box, which was unfortunate for me in that I'd need to turn my head if I wanted to look at him as he spoke, a gesture he and his team would undoubtedly notice. I resolved to focus my gaze only on the judge in front of me and resist all attempts to turn away or look behind.

The Claimant was the absolute picture of a pathetic, sick,

elderly and utterly helpless person as he sat there, adjacent to his brief, wheezing and spluttering into his oxygen mask and clutching an inhaler in his right fist as if his very life depended upon it. He took his oath on the Bible and swore, by Almighty God, to tell the truth. I felt pretty certain that the words were hollow and meaningless to him and I sincerely doubted he had any kind of religious belief at all. Still, it looked good, him taking the oath as a god-fearing and decent man, didn't it? Very much aware that he intended for the court and everyone present to see him as the injured party in this affair, I turned my eyes away and looked at the judge as he invited David Price, my QC, to begin his cross-examination.

Evidently, the Claimant had hearing issues because a great deal of what David said in the run-up to each question was apparently unintelligible and so the esteemed gentleman was for the most part unable to hear or comprehend almost everything David said. This was such a puerile attempt at delay and obstruction that I could barely keep a frustrated sneer from my own face; it must have been far more irritating for David who had the need to repeat and rephrase almost every word he uttered. After about half an hour or so of this, the judge himself intervened and made it abundantly clear what exactly David wanted to know, to which the Claimant feigned comprehension and made a strong play of telling the judge that he could understand everything he said perfectly well but that he could 'barely hear' David (who was considerably closer to him). Such smarmy remarks and ham acting were so undignified and inappropriate in that august environment that

I couldn't help a brief shake of my head. I have no idea how the judge retained his neutral expression. Personally, had I been the judge, I'd have had the Claimant and his team hauled out of the room for contempt – something I strongly felt should happen anyhow because the whole case was plainly a vindictive move meant to try to frighten me, and probably other people too, into keeping silent about incidents from the past which had caused them fear, humiliation, shame or grief.

Whilst the Claimant had a short break in order to go to the lavatory, my mind wandered once more and I found myself fervently wishing, not for the first time, that I had kept silent about incidents from the past, my past anyhow. All of this, the hours of preparation and gathering of witness statements, investigation and so on by my own team, never mind the Claimant's lot, the resources used up, time consumed, expenditure incurred, attention garnered, all of it could have been avoided if I'd only kept schtum. Why on earth hadn't I kept my big mouth shut? I wondered for the nth time. On the other hand, why had he (the Claimant) so confidently and vehemently denied ever having been at the BBC or on a show hosted by the National Treasure – Jimmy Savile – when the 'awful allegations' I'd made had come to light? So confident was he that I'd lied about him he had taken out an injunction in order to prevent what I'd said being broadcast or reported. Obviously, he had no memory whatsoever of the event. Why should he? I couldn't recall most of the evening myself, only the part that related directly to me, how he'd smelled just like my stepfather and had humiliated me utterly in front of my peers and several strangers when I'd overreacted to being goosed by him.

The morning progressed and, to me, time slowed to a crawl. David asked his questions, the Claimant appeared to be unable to hear or understand every single one before making any kind of reply, often going off the subject matter of the question and needing to be redirected back to it by the judge himself. There were multiple breaks whilst he used his inhaler, took his medication, had coughing fits and so on. Certainly, he gave a strong impression that he was gravely unwell and that being in court affected him adversely. Of course, that would be my fault I mused, as I tried not to be disrespectful to the court by overtly yawning or dozing off to sleep. Fairly early on in the questioning, the Claimant had answered to something David asked by snapping an irritable reply to the effect that he didn't know because he'd never been in court before. David had pounced on this statement straight away; I'd easily detected the triumphant lilt in David's incredulous tone as he challenged the remark. This had been the first obvious untruth. There were to be many, many more.

At first, the Claimant said he'd 'forgotten' that he'd done the *Clunk Click* show with the National Treasure in early March of 1974. He went on at some length, practically bragging that he did so many shows (he mentioned somewhere in the region of twenty thousand) he could hardly be expected to recall them all. Under further questioning, he insisted that what I'd said couldn't possibly have happened because he never, ever stayed behind after shows; apparently, he'd had somewhere else to go immediately after the show ended. I'm certain I wasn't the only person in the room who wondered how he could recall that detail so very clearly when he hadn't actually been able to recall doing the show in the first place! The questions came, one after another, and my adversary floundered in his replies, sometimes contradicting himself even in the same sentence. I thought it must be abundantly clear to everyone, not just to me, that this whole case was a complete waste of time and money.

When the Claimant suddenly remarked that his wife had been with him on the show, my mouth briefly dropped open in unconcealed astonishment. He went on to add that, not only had his spouse been with him throughout the recording and both prior to and after the show had finished, but also his manager. Apparently, his ex-wife couldn't come to court because her present husband wouldn't let her get involved in the case. I knew this to be complete rubbish of course; after all, I had an unwilling witness myself whom I'd had to subpoena to appear. David asked, whilst keeping his tone mild and only slightly curious, as to whether the Claimant intended to call his ex-manager to give evidence and added that in all the pre-prepared and exchanged paperwork and documents there had been no mention of either his wife or his manager. I completely forgot that I'd resolved not to turn in my seat and turned to look my accuser when he snarled a furious, muttered oath in reply.

David then began to ask about women and the Claimant's attitude towards them, particularly to the younger women he encountered. I stared at the intricate grain of the oak table in front of me as I listened to the Claimant describe how he liked women and had an extremely high sex drive. He sat there in his wheelchair, apparently struggling to breathe, and bragged, yes, bragged, that he'd needed to have sexual intercourse eight or more times a day back in the 1970s. Clearly unimpressed, David asked about the Claimant's obvious preference for younger ladies. I'd not have been in the least surprised had he denied this but, again, in a bragging manner, he agreed that, whilst he did like younger women, he 'drew the line' at about twenty-two years of age. He had no interest whatever, he said, in females under the age of around twenty-two.

I had to keep a firm hold on myself; I didn't want to be seen by the judge and the reporters to show my incredulity at what I (and the rest of the court) was hearing. Although everything about the evening to which I'd referred in my memoirs was hazy, I could recall that the Claimant, then a young, trendy-looking and reasonably attractive man, had behaved like a kid let loose in a sweet shop. However, this particular line of questioning wasn't about what I remembered; it was wholly about what (if anything) the Claimant himself recalled of the event, which was very obviously almost nothing.

By lunchtime, I felt sick to death of the sound of the Claimant's voice and his constant complaints of being unable to either hear David properly or comprehend what he might be 'getting at'. Although we had in fact only been seated for around three hours, it felt like very much longer to me as I stood, along with everybody else, while the judge rose and left the room. I felt stiff and achy, incredibly tired and more than eager for a cup of hot tea. David and Helen led Peter and me out of the courtroom and to a different staircase than the main one by which we'd entered. David remarked that he felt certain the judge must feel insulted by the manner in which the Claimant was behaving and added that, in his opinion, sucking up to the judge was a foolish error to make and would certainly not distract this particular judge from the facts. Helen told us to ensure we were back in court by two o'clock, and then, at the entrance to the Royal Courts of Justice building, we went our separate ways.

Peter went to a cash machine and I waited nearby. A photographer walking past suddenly stopped in his tracks and stepped back, pointing a huge lens in my direction. I raised my arm to cover my face and tried to turn away, but the photographer simply moved as well and continued taking photographs. Eventually, he made some remark about it being better to let him get a picture or two because then he could leave me in peace and so I dropped my arm and glared, stony-faced, into the lens whilst the man took about a dozen or more pictures. He thanked me, although I felt so furious I couldn't summon my voice to reply. The fellow didn't appear to notice and hurried away, evidently searching for more people to harass with his blasted camera. Without a word, Peter steered me into a nearby Pret A Manger where we joined the queue.

Nobody took a bit of notice of either of us as we purchased our lunch and found somewhere to sit. It felt absolutely marvellous to me to have once more slipped into a more normal, insignificant and unremarkable role and I relaxed enough to be able to eat my sandwich and drink the longed-for tea. As a qualified nurse and my carer, as well being one of the very few people I actually trust, Peter really had his work cut out in keeping me balanced and reasonably relaxed. The lunch break passed all too rapidly and Peter remarked that we'd need to get back to the court. That was the first time he'd mentioned the word throughout our break; our conversation had been about small, insignificant and unimportant things, such as the choice of sandwich fillings on offer to the problem of finding an alternative hotel in which to stay due to there being no elevator in our current one. I felt pathetically grateful for this small consideration, although I didn't remark on it.

When we returned to the court, microphones had been set up and the clerk was busy adjusting them. No one else had returned from the break yet and so, aside from the clerk, Peter and I were the only people in the room. I remarked on the carving and the woodwork, and then the ceiling. To my surprise, the clerk turned and smiled at us. 'You should take the opportunity, if you get it, to go down the corridor and have a look at Court Fourteen. It is fabulous and much more ornate than this one.'

She went on to tell us a little about the building's history and how every individual courtroom was different and unique. The brief and interesting conversation was cut short by other people returning to the room, including the Claimant and his team, the press and two or three others who had not been present – or at least, I hadn't noticed them – earlier in the day.

Chapter Four

Location: Ludham village, Norfolk

Timeline: *circa* 1965–9

perpetrator: *noun*: 'One who commits a criminal, violent or hurtful act.'

My new 'daddy' was just another grown-up who didn't like me – or so I thought at first. It quickly turned out that, in fact, he didn't mind taking my knickers off, throwing me across his knee and thrashing my little bottom with his bare hand whilst I screamed and writhed in agony. Mother would watch these hidings at first, either completely impassive or with a triumphant sneer on her face. After we had all lived together in the horrible little hovel in Ludham for a few months, Mother appeared to lose interest in watching. Her favourite phrase was 'Just you wait until your father gets home.' Commonly, just as soon as my stepfather crossed the threshold when he returned from work, Mother launched into a tirade of my multiple crimes that day by way of greeting. He took to snatching me up by the back of whatever clothing I happened to be wearing at the time and would then stomp up the narrow, steep staircase, dragging me upwards behind him. Once he'd crossed the bedroom he shared with Mother and ducked through the narrow doorway into what passed as a bedroom for me, he'd hurl me across the narrow patch of bare boards between the doorway and my little bed before the thrashing began. In the little kitchen beneath my room, Mother would have been able to hear my shrieks and screams clearly as she prepared my stepfather's meal.

At about the same time as we moved into the hovel in Ludham, I'd had to begin attending the local primary school. Ordinarily, this wouldn't be a major problem for a child – other than perhaps, for more normal children, separation anxiety – but for me it was simply torturous. I'd been completely isolated from the company of other children up until the day I began school. In fact, I don't believe I'd ever even noticed that other children existed before attending.

Although it was only a small local primary school, to me, aged about five and a half, the place seemed huge and daunting. Within a minute of my walking through the gate, I was marked out as 'different' because when another adult approached Mother and me, not only could I not understand what she said in her thick Norfolk accent, but when Mother nudged me between the shoulder blades and ordered me to say hello and tell the lady my name it seemed as if everything else – general chatter, children running about, adults talking – ceased and all attention turned to me. Feeling like a rabbit caught in headlights, although I could never have articulated that particular feeling back then, of course, I enunciated my name carefully and clearly, adding 'hello' afterwards... and all the kids roared with laughter. Some pointed and giggled, others just sniggered and turned back to their friends and the games they'd been playing; the teacher frowned and I knew that, somehow, I'd managed to make new enemies, but I couldn't even begin to fathom how or why.

Everybody at the school spoke with a pronounced Norfolk accent, which effectively camouflaged their words enough to make me unable to decipher what they might be saying. In fact, had they all spoken French, Italian or Martian, I'd have been just as baffled. Teachers told me what to do and asked questions of me and I, apparently, ignored them. During break times, a few children tried to goad me to speak but, whenever I did, they pointed and laughed at me. In a matter of a few days I learned to remain absolutely silent; I sat at my allotted desk, hanging my head so as not to catch the eye of any child who might be looking my way. I dreaded having to utter anything out loud, and so parrot-style chanting of times tables was an awful experience.

I'm almost certain the school was responsible for my regression in toilet training; either that or it really was pure fear that caused me to wet my knickers so often. Very rapidly the other kids began to vie with one another to see who could make the posh girl piss her pants the quickest. Mother, on being presented with my soggy underwear at home-time most days, decided this was yet another ploy of mine undertaken deliberately in order to humiliate and discredit her. It was a thrashable offence too, so, before I'd even left the school every day, I knew I'd get a slap in the face from Mother, a stream of abuse screeched at me and that, as soon as my stepfather returned from work, another spanking would be on the cards.

My stepfather absolutely hated my tendency to urinate when frightened. He also did not, apparently, recognise this as a fear response but believed it to be something I did deliberately in order to try to avoid the thrashing. He certainly stopped flinging me across his knees, if only because his trousers would then need to be laundered. Instead, he used one huge, grimy hand to pin me down – either on the bed or the floor – and the other to spank me with. Of course, I generally began to scream 'No! No! No!' as soon as he entered the house, but by the time the actual thrashing had begun my screams were wordless.

Mother took to stripping off my clothing as soon as we got home after school; it was the only way, I suppose, she could ensure that it remained wearable the following day. Of course, she coldly informed me that she didn't then want to have to see me lounging about naked and so, after a drink of water and sometimes a jam sandwich, I'd be sent to bed. Naturally, my stepfather still came stamping up the narrow staircase and I'd generally wet the bed or the floor long before he flung open the door to my small room.

On the day I was attacked at school by a big boy who tended to throw his weight about and often clouted other kids, I was far too terrified of him to attempt to tell the teacher why I rolled about on the playground screaming in agony. The boy had dragged me off the climbing frame by my hair and kicked me in between my legs when I reflexively lashed out at him. Of course, I wet myself, as usual. The teacher took me to the office, but I resolutely refused to tell her what had occurred even though my sobbing and wailing had pretty much rendered me speechless anyhow. When Mother came to collect me that day I stood miserably beside my red-faced parent who was, quite clearly, mortified at receiving more attention due to my behaviour and listened listlessly as the teacher said she had not been able to establish what had happened. Much of what the woman said was unintelligible to me because of her accent, but I did catch the word 'attention' – Mother always accused me of trying to draw attention to myself, whatever that meant – and, with my heart descending into my ugly school shoes, I knew I'd be in for yet another hiding.

It hurt to walk, which was another crime as far as Mother was concerned. She dragged me along by the shoulder of my coat ignoring both my sobs and pleas for her to stop and the glances of enquiry from other people. I got two hard smacks across my face once she'd shoved me inside the house and slammed the door. She practically tore my clothing off and, eager to get me out of her sight, screeched at me to get upstairs to bed. I scuttled up the stairs and into my little room and, once I'd wrapped myself in the bedspread, only slightly damp and smelly from where I had wet myself the previous evening, I hugged Lambie as I rocked back and forth trying to comfort myself somewhat. Weeping, trembling and screaming are high-energy pastimes and I fell asleep. However, I soon woke when my door crashed open and banged against the wall. My

31

stepfather stood there, hunched over so as not to strike his head as he entered the room – not that he was particularly tall, the doorway was just very small – and with an expression on his face of undisguised disgust.

Rather than striding forward as he usually did, he entered the room and stood upright, hands on hips, and demanded to know what I had thought I was doing at school, drawing attention to myself and refusing to tell anybody why I was making such a disturbance and fuss. I huddled inside the bedspread and tried not to shake too hard. I don't know what my facial expression showed but whatever it was, my stepfather took great offence and back-handed me with a loud shout, something about insolence. Of course, my bladder played its usual trick but, wrapped as I was, he didn't notice. It probably took about half an hour of threats, slaps, a sound tooth-rattling shaking, lots of shouting and, lastly, being dragged from my huddle and flung naked to the floor before I found my voice and yelled, between sobs, 'A big boy kicked me!' My stepfather actually lifted me up by a skinny ankle and made an exaggerated inspection of my scrawny body as he sneered that he could see no bruises, and so I must be lying. He dropped me back to the floor and raised his arm to begin the thrashing so long delayed but I shouted, 'Here! He hurt me here!' and pointed to my crotch. He made some sarcastic, mean comment along the lines of my being a bit young to be such a slut before he stared at that area of my body for what seemed like ages... and then moved suddenly with rattlesnake speed.

That first penetration made me retch; I'd never experienced

such pain in my life before, despite all the hidings I'd had from him and Mother. He wiped his hands on the bedspread before he left the room and, through my tears, I saw blood, although that was the least of my concerns because I actually feared vomiting above all else and I couldn't stop retching. I still retched hard the next morning whilst Mother dressed me for school. Mother hated to deal with vomit and so retching was the very worst thing I could do and earned me a ringing slap around the ear. I couldn't eat any breakfast and I could barely walk when it came time to leave for school. Mother dragged me whilst silent tears spilled down my cheeks.

School remained as awful as ever although I was not assaulted very often, not physically anyhow. The main entertainment for the other kids, of all ages, was who could say or do something to make the girl, who insisted on staying posh and 'speaking funny', to wet her knickers. Sometimes the teacher won that contest, generally by saying she'd be telling my mother about whatever crime I'd allegedly committed. Almost every day involved having my face or ears slapped by Mother before being stripped naked and sent to bed. My stepfather always came straight upstairs when he arrived home from work. Sometimes he only shouted and thrashed me. There were other, darker times, when what he did caused me to bleed and writhe with pain all night long, holding my woollen lamb close to my face for what little comfort it offered.

Chapter Five

Location: Court 13, Royal Courts of Justice, Strand, London

Timeline: 16 June 2015 – day two of the case

witness: *noun*: 1. 'An individual who, being present, personally sees or perceives a thing; a beholder, spectator or eyewitness.' 2. 'A person who gives testimony, as in a court of law.'

I watched Susan Bunce move to the witness stand. She still had the same walk; she looked almost the same as she had forty years or so ago – well, perhaps she'd lost a little weight and her blonde hair had darkened somewhat – and I had a sensation, in my upper abdomen, as if my heart had flipped a somersault within me. What nobody knew was that I'd had quite the crush on Susan Bunce when we were at Duncroft together. She was everything I'd always longed to be: petite, feminine, beautiful, confident and, despite being slender, had a pronounced bust. The fact that the girl was detached and remained aloof to everyone and, apparently, everything, had been something else I'd admired about her. I used to watch Susan move about the room and wish fervently that I could be like her. I so wanted her to like me; the few times she'd smiled at me I felt lighter than air. For some reason, most of the other Duncroft girls didn't seem to like Susan very much. They disliked me intensely, that much I already knew and, having spent my entire life being avoided, disliked and made fun of, this was nothing new. However, it puzzled me as to why they picked on Susan a lot of the time.

For all that I admired the girl, now a woman, I can remember very little of her during our time at Duncroft; she often just didn't appear in my memories at all. I wondered if that meant my memories were somehow deficient – entirely possible – or whether there had been some other reason for my not being able to recall her being present much of the time. I do remember that she went home most weekends.

Helen believed I was supposed to be intimidated by Susan having been called as a witness by the Claimant. Apparently, unlike me, Susan could recall the evening at the BBC Theatre in Shepherds Bush forty years previously in perfect detail and this fact was meant to make me tremble in my boots. I can't say I trembled as I sat there looking at the woman I'd have sold my soul to be like, but I did feel somewhat wistful as I glanced down at my massive feet and huge hands. I leaned close to Helen and whispered, 'You know, I had a dreadful crush on her when we were at Duncroft.' Helen raised her brows at this revelation but, if she judged me, she kept it to herself. Somehow, simply by admitting how I used to feel around Susan Bunce, I no longer felt it.

David began his cross-examination. I felt more engaged and interested in what Susan had to say than in anything the

Claimant had uttered the previous day and so I paid close attention to everything she said. I discovered first-hand how Susan had first met Jimmy Savile: her mother owned, or managed, a country club and Susan, being at home for the weekend and due to staff shortages, was helping her mother there one evening. The need for Susan to appear older than her fifteen years meant that her mother had permitted her to wear more make-up than usual for the occasion. Jimmy Savile had been one of the club's guests that evening and had taken a shine to Susan.

I listened, aghast, as Susan calmly spoke of how Savile had wanted to see her again. She described, in detail, the artful and manipulative grooming of her unsuspecting parents, who permitted her to go off on her own with Savile the following day. Evidently, this apparently intelligent woman did not recognise any of what she related as having been odd, inappropriate, peculiar, or that she and her parents had been victims of one of the most prolific sexual predators this country had ever exposed. She described how, after drinking tea, she went with Savile, upstairs to his bedroom where they lay down, side by side, on his bed. She told the court how just before she'd set out from home she'd taken some 'acid' or LSD, and went on to describe how the drug was affecting her as she lay there beside Savile. Realising that the girl was stoned, Savile did not molest her; oh no, he simply masturbated, right there beside her, whilst her mind was off with the fairies. She stated she'd been well aware of what he was doing, but she didn't seem to think, even now, that there was anything wrong with it. He then took her back downstairs and made her drink tea until she'd recovered. He was vociferous in his condemnation of drug-taking and Susan felt anxious that he might not want to see her again. She felt quite certain that he thought she was a lot older than fifteen and hesitated to tell him, when he asked her to come out with him another time, that she had to return to school – namely Duncroft. In fact, when she did tell him about Duncroft, he beamed at her and promised to visit her there as her 'special friend'.

I'm pretty certain I wasn't the only person sitting in that courtroom who recognised the description of Savile's behaviour for what it was and his instant eagerness to visit her at her school as a terrible threat. The thought sent shivers down my spine and I felt momentarily nauseous, not least because I'd already met Savile myself before going to Duncroft, and I had worried, in the absence of memory, whether it had been my fault that he'd gone there to prey upon vulnerable and damaged girls. To hear Susan relate, matter-of-factly, how it had come about and that he had followed her (rather than me) gave me both enlightenment and relief. As Susan continued to speak, answering David's questions, and as the story of how Savile had visited Duncroft frequently – always bearing gifts, which he showered upon the girls – unfolded, little snippets of memory appeared in my mind and then sank away again, much as vegetables might rise to the surface and sink again in a simmering pot of soup. I felt distinctly physically uncomfortable and, as David progressed to questioning Susan about the evening at the BBC Theatre, when a group of us, as guests of Savile, had met the Claimant, those feelings of discomfort increased. I knew I'd begun to perspire heavily again despite the air-conditioning in the courtroom and could only hope it wasn't too obvious to the reporters who kept glancing at me, and moreover, that I didn't smell too bad.

Susan had a particular way of describing the female toilet. She used the phrase 'The ladies' WC', which, to my mind, was extremely old-fashioned and the kind of descriptor my grandmother might have used. She told the court she had been on the way back from a visit to said WC when she encountered the Claimant in the corridor. They had struck up a conversation and he walked with her to the room where we were all gathered. She went on to describe the filming of the show and how she and the other Duncroft girls had all sat on the stage on large coloured beanbags, together with several other young people. She explained that Miss Theobold and Miss Jones had been sent to sit in the audience – something I had entirely forgotten but which explained why they were not present during and after filming.

I recalled that, after the filming had finished, all of Savile's guests had returned to his dressing room where a party atmosphere prevailed. The BBC had provided 'hospitality' and, as I recalled things, this included both plates of finger food and a great variety of drinks, mostly alcoholic but also soft drinks and coffee. Susan described nothing of the kind; she mentioned that she'd gone to the WC (again) and, when she had returned, was startled to hear that she had missed out on food, drink and even cigarettes, and did not believe the other girls when they told her. She described how the Claimant had lifted her into the air and swung her around in a circle, her golden hair flying and that, whilst she was giggling, one of the Duncroft girls called out something like, 'Why don't you kiss him?' and she had done so. This was not a peck on the cheek or any type of chaste kiss but a full-on, lingering French kiss. She assured David that the Claimant was in no way to blame for the kiss because she had instigated it and it was all included in the general light-hearted and heady atmosphere of the gathering. She didn't mind in the least, she said, and therefore, it was perfectly acceptable.

David pointed out, yet again, that she was in fact younger than me by some six months and so it was very definitely not acceptable for a man in his early thirties to be publicly French-kissing a schoolgirl. Susan tried very hard to persuade David and the rest of those present in the court that there was no way the Claimant would have known how young she was. She claimed to have made every effort to distance herself from the other Duncroft girls and, by simple omission, lead the Claimant to believe she was over eighteen. Of course, a few minutes later she described having gone to the WC yet again, and upon her return, noticed all the Duncroft girls smoking Marlboro cigarettes which the Claimant had allegedly given them. She went on to tell David that she joined the group to ask for a cigarette for herself – which the Claimant indicated she should take out of his pocket – which rather spoiled the idea that she was nothing to do with Duncroft. Also, she told David how the Claimant kept offering her a lift home, saying his car and driver were outside and he would take her anywhere she liked.

By the time David got round to the part of the evening that involved me and the allegation I'd made, the Claimant's team had begun to look more than a little flustered. Obviously, this was not at all how Susan's evidence had been supposed to go, for she had made it abundantly clear that, despite what he'd said, the Claimant was clearly interested in very young girls – although he'd said in his own evidence the previous day that he 'drew the line' at the age of about twenty-two. I found myself variously amazed at Susan's clarity of recall and suspicious as to what she might say about me. Still, there was nothing I could do about it; so far, she'd told the truth and I could only hope she continued to do so.

In fact, as Susan described what she had witnessed, my heart rattled against the inside of my ribs and I felt vaguely sick. She said that she hadn't seen the Claimant actually touch me but she had seen him, from across the room, approach me. She elaborated, when asked to by David: the other girls had been taunting me, she told the court, about my old-fashioned clothing and the way I looked; one of the girls had called out to the Claimant, 'She wants to know if you'd fancy her' or something similar, in the hope that his attention would embarrass me. She added that, although she certainly didn't see him put his hands on me, she saw me suddenly start waving my arms about and making a fuss, whilst repeating 'Don't touch me!' Although she said she couldn't recall the Claimant himself saying anything by way of reply, she did agree that everyone had laughed and she'd realised I was mortified by the episode. Susan had told the truth and nothing more; whether or not she meant to do so, she had backed up my account absolutely! I glanced across at the Claimant and his team and saw him snarling with fury. As Susan stepped down from the witness box at lunchtime, I overheard the Claimant say, amongst other things, 'They're all lying bitches, old school tie and all that. They've probably been in touch these last forty years and concocted all these lies to discredit me.'

I tried to maintain a blank countenance but, in all truth, I was turning his words over and over in my head. Did he really believe I'd kept in touch for more than forty years with people who'd hated me? Or that I'd nothing better with which to fill my empty little life than cooking up a conspiracy to discredit him? In a way, it almost meant he'd admitted doing me wrong, for no sane person would conspire with others and go out of their way to discredit someone without reason. Yet, he didn't think I was sane, did he? I recalled the telephone conversation with the reporter who'd contacted me about many of the things the Claimant had said during his Wolverhampton gig, shortly after my television interview had been broadcast in early October 2012. She'd told me he'd described me as 'a nutter', amongst other things. Somehow, he'd looked into me and my antecedents, seen the train-wreck I called a life, and shared my personal disorders, failures and multiple disasters with a live audience – who'd laughed. Of course, the actual truth – that I hadn't actually tried to discredit him; I'd merely mentioned that something cruel he'd said had humiliated me utterly and that I'd carried the sting of his casual cruelty for most of my adult life – didn't appear to matter. This whole case had surely been brought for no other reason than to completely discredit me and everything I'd written or said, which seemed odd since I'd not asked him for compensation, or indeed anything at all – not even an apology, although he'd demanded I apologise to him – and I certainly had absolutely nothing whatever to gain by inventing what I'd said.

During the break for lunch, I kept my feelings firmly to myself, although I knew Peter was aware that my mind remained firmly in that courtroom, picking over everything Susan had said so far. In fact, as we ate our lunch with playwright and broadcaster Jonny Maitland, who had popped along to see how things were going, Peter remarked that he thought I was weathering the ordeal extremely well so far and Jonny gave a shout of laughter. His eyes twinkled as he remarked – with his mouth full of salad – that he'd been constantly amazed and in awe of my resilience ever since he'd first seen me on the television. I never know how to deal with compliments at the best of times and so I ducked my head and muttered something about it all happening in spite of me; short of lie down and die, I just had to face it and continue blundering on through to the end. We didn't discuss anything that had actually been said inside the courtroom but went on to talk about Jonny's play, about how Savile had manipulated a whole nation, not just a few kids. The play was doing extremely well.

I went to use the main courthouse toilets before ascending the stairs back to court and, as I left the cubicle, I encountered

Susan washing her hands. There were only two basins and I couldn't avoid her, and so, forcing my face into a somewhat strained smile, I greeted her: 'Hello, stranger.'

She turned to face me, having wiped her hands dry and replied, 'I'm not supposed to talk to you, but I do care, you know.' She hurried away, leaving me standing over the basin staring at myself in the ancient mirror, with my heart inexplicably thundering like an erratic bass drum in my own ears.

Chapter Six

dead: *adjective*: 'No longer alive.'
gone: *adjective*: 'No longer present; departed.'

L iving in the tiny terraced cottage in Ludham with Mother and my new daddy was terrible, as was having to go to the village school every weekday, and I was desperately unhappy and very, very frightened almost all of the time. However, weekends were slightly less unpleasant because they generally involved visiting grandparents. Of course, I already visited Nana regularly, usually without my parents. Mother often took me to Nana's house and then went off, to do 'grown-up things', Nana said. I didn't mind at all. I felt safe and loved when I was with Nana at Gable Cottage.

That I had suddenly acquired more grandparents didn't strike me as particularly strange. I was only five years old and so, I suppose, accepted this kind of thing without question. I liked Nanny and Grandad well enough and they were both kind to me. Nanny always seemed to be wearing a flowery apron which covered her from ample bosom to knee. She also seemed to exist exclusively within a fragrant, mouth-watering haze of mixed foods in various stages of construction; she was forever baking, roasting, chopping and mincing. When she left the steamy confines of the kitchen those scents lingered on her and, to my childish mind, even followed her. Grandad, on the other hand, spent most of his time in his vegetable garden. There were interesting and intriguing smells out there too, not to mention the big black family dog with the permanently wagging tail.

I'd managed to acquire a 'Great-Nanny' too: a frail, wizened old lady, with a shock of pure white, frizzy hair, which made determined attempts to escape from her desperately old-fashioned mob-cap. She lived in the front parlour – which had been converted to a bed-sitting room for her exclusive use – and I was encouraged to sit with her in order to occupy and entertain her with my childish chatter. I used to perch on a footstool right beside her chair and chant my times tables or nursery rhymes; sometimes, she'd put her liver-spotted, wrinkly and arthritic hand gently on my head as she smiled and nodded.

I was sitting on that stool beside her on the day she died. The death rattle caused me to look at her in alarm and I saw she was drooling. Unable to rouse the old dear, I fled into the kitchen, through the sitting room where Mother sat, reading a magazine, and screamed at Nanny that there was something ever so wrong with Great-Nanny. Nanny and my new daddy hurried through to the front parlour with alarm writ large on their faces, but Mother didn't move save to lower her book and glare at me before she accused me of having done something to the old lady. I felt inexplicably frightened, and when Mother further informed me, from between clenched teeth, that the old woman had better be all right or something really dire would be happening to me by way of punishment, panic filled me and I very nearly wet myself there and then. When Nanny came back into the room and shook her head as she told Mother that Great-Nanny was dead and that Daddy had gone to the phone box down the road to call the doctor, I raced outside to the garden instantly terrified of what punishment Mother might mete out.

Of course, I had no idea what 'dead' meant but I remember wondering if it hurt and how one might get better from it. I asked Grandad about it and added that Great-Nanny had it and he dropped his fork and ran indoors without answering my question; it was all extremely curious. I never saw the old woman again, which was even more peculiar. Mother kept saying it had all been my fault, but Nanny and Grandad never said anything like that to me.

Some few weeks after this event, I was astonished when Nana arrived one morning and Mother remained upstairs. Another lady came; she looked very strict and severe and complained angrily when I opened the door, so that poor Matty the dog raced upstairs to be with Mother, who cried out several times. Now and then I heard Mother scream and the sounds frightened me witless. I couldn't think of anything that might make my big, scary parent scream like that and I couldn't stop shaking either. I tried, unsuccessfully, to hide. Nana attempted to soothe me, telling me everything would be fine, it was just the baby coming (although what that might mean or where this baby thing was coming from and why it made Mother scream so loudly she didn't explain).

Nana became very busy, boiling water in pots and the kettle and doing stuff with buckets and towels. However, she still found the time to make me a small picnic and she sent me outside to sit on a soft blanket and share it with my dollies. Actually, I hated all those dollies (except Billy) because they all had the same ice-blue eyes as Mother and they always stared at me. I treated them very much in the same way as Mother treated me – meaning I smacked their faces and their bottoms repeatedly, shouted at them, pulled their hair and snarled the same spiteful words Mother directed at me regularly. Whilst my mother struggled to give birth upstairs in the tiny terraced hovel, I smashed one doll's face in with a lump of rock because she wouldn't stop staring at me, and her cold glare, coupled with the still audible screams from within, thoroughly unnerved and frightened me. When Nana and the severe woman came outside to speak to me about a new baby brother and saw what I'd done, the woman told Nana to ensure I was never left alone with the baby, not even for a few seconds, because if I treated the baby in even a tiny way as badly as I treated my dolls, I'd kill him. Nana took me upstairs after the strict lady had left, to see Mother who was sitting up in bed holding something small and ugly in a soft blue blanket. Quite suddenly, my life changed yet again, although I was never allowed to touch the baby. I'd hear Mother singing softly to him from my tiny little room upstairs. I didn't like the baby much because he screamed nearly all night long, made the whole place stink of poo and sick and was the reason every room contained nappies in varying conditions: wet, soiled, soaking, drying.

Sad to say, this major change also coincided with a particularly tough time I experienced at school. I'd managed, by some mysterious means, to fall foul of a big girl who had the task of cleaning tables at lunchtimes. She'd wipe her stinking cloth in my face whenever she could, which made me retch, thus putting me off my food. This in turn caused me to come into contention with the fierce dinner ladies, who insisted food must be eaten up and not wasted. Playtime became a thing of the past because I was forced to remain at table all through the break whilst those well-intentioned women tried to physically shove the food into my mouth. Most days still found me stripped out of my school wear and sent to my room as soon as I got home, although Daddy didn't always come to thrash me or hurt my bottom in other ways.

Probably the only pleasant events in my life at that time were my regular visits to Nana in her little cottage. But, well before the beginning of the school summer holidays, those visits ceased abruptly. There was no explanation for this or any kind of reassurance. I began to wonder if Nana had got dead somehow, although I felt pretty certain I hadn't given it to her like I had Great-Nanny. Eventually, screwing my courage tightly, I slunk down the stairs and shuffled into the kitchen, where Mother was scrubbing nappies at the sink, and asked her if Nana was dead. Her reaction was extreme to say the least: she went completely crazy and accused me of wanting her beloved mother to die! She slapped at every part of me with her huge, wet hands and further accused me of all manner of wickedness. Of course, I yelled and wept and tried to escape but the blows continued to rain down upon me along with terrible shrieked threats. She only stopped because the baby woke up – that was my fault too. When I finally escaped the thrashing and curled on my little bed I did so knowing that Nana hadn't got dead but she had gone, although where or for how long, or what the difference might be, I still had no clue.

Evidently I was not important enough to have anything explained to me, so the move, when it happened a couple of weeks later, became another trauma that I didn't understand. Mother got very tearful because we had to leave Matty behind with Grandad because we were travelling by train. The unexpected exodus was scary but also exciting and, despite Mother's mean and spiteful remarks and the way she shook me off like something foul when I tried to hold onto her hand, I was enthralled once we reached the great station in Norwich by the huge trains and carriages, trolleys full of luggage and throngs of people on the station concourse. I spent the journey with my nose pressed against the carriage window watching town and countryside flash by.

We ended up at Liverpool Street station in London, which was an even more massive edifice. I strained my neck looking up and around in wonder and nearly got lost as my parents hurried to the exit. We were met by a small, stout fellow who strongly resembled Nana; he turned out to be Nana's elder brother – or one of them – so that made him my great-uncle. He loaded all of us and our luggage into his car and drove us, for what felt like hours, to Mornington Road, Chingford, where I was profoundly delighted and relieved to be reunited with Nana. For a few days we all stayed with Nana in her spacious upstairs flat in a large house. Nana's disabled sister (my great-aunt) lived in the downstairs portion of the house along with her husband. After just a couple of days, Mother, Daddy and the baby went off somewhere, leaving me staying on my own with Nana. I couldn't have been happier and I hoped that would be the way things would stay.

The day Nana took me with her on the bus across Chingford to Forest Side – then a long road with houses and flats on one side of the road and the mature trees of Epping Forest lining the other – I thought we were just going on an outing. Nana did tell me we were going to see Mummy, Daddy and the baby, but she didn't make it clear to me that I would be remaining there with them whilst she returned alone to Mornington Road. Although the flat was more spacious, brighter and cleaner than the old place in Ludham, not to mention having been newly decorated throughout, I wept inconsolably when Nana left. After putting up with my sobbing for around ten minutes, Daddy gave me something to cry for – namely a darned good thrashing – and shut me in the bedroom I was to share with my baby brother.

The abuse and torture I endured whilst living in that flat formed the framework upon which the miserable, terrified and lonely little girl I would become evolved. Mother worked nights at the London Rubber Company and Daddy took full advantage of her absence. His nightly ritual occurred, for the most part, in the bathroom; my 'stinking fanny' had to be washed, by me, in a certain way, whilst standing in the bath, using both Mother's face flannel and her perfumed soap, which stung and irritated the severe eczema patches in my groin area, itself causing me to sob in agony. At first, I learned how to masturbate the adult penis but, eventually, this inevitably progressed to learning to fellate without either vomiting or gagging (for which the punishment was a jug of water or two being emptied over my head causing me to scream and panic, immediately followed by a sound thrashing). Daddy hurt my bottom during those times too and I became even more terrified of water than I'd been before.

Once or twice, Daddy brought the neighbours into the house to watch, incredulous, the way in which I behaved at the very mention of the word 'bath' – the kicking and screaming, struggling and pleading for mercy, the tears and begging those neighbours to intervene and 'save me'. On one occasion, Daddy had been talking to his friends and I'd been sitting quietly in the corner with Lambie. He fetched the big jug from the bathroom and set it on the table... just so his audience could watch the way I reacted.

Children seem to know, instinctively, who to avoid, and it is a very sad fact, even today, that those kids who suffer abuse and neglect, constant haranguing rather than praise, scorn rather than affection, threats of violence or ridicule rather than encouragement, do not make friends easily. In fact, they tend to be, at best, ignored, but more often bullied by their peers as well as those who should be caring for them, protecting and shielding them. So I would become. I had no idea how to form friendships or how to decide who would be trustworthy and who not. In short, I was always very unpopular, but at the same time, in many ways I became incredibly thick-skinned about the fact that others appeared to dislike or even hate me. For as long as I remained within my family where unspeakable events continued to occur, no matter where we lived or which schools I attended, the results were always the same: I was thoroughly shunned – except by men, who desired my company and attention (and all the demands that went with it, of course). I didn't truly comprehend the extent of my long-term isolation and loneliness until I was well into adulthood and, in fact, on the other side of a total breakdown.

That I arrived, as a teenager in 1973, at Duncroft, 'Home Office Approved School for Intelligent but Emotionally Disturbed Girls' in Staines, it might have been the saving of me, except that no one believed what I told them about my stepfather and the way Mother had always treated me. I told so many people in positions of authority who I believed were obliged or duty bound to help me make the horror stop, but Mother and her husband were far better at lying than I was at explaining the horrendous truth. Although I cannot claim to have suddenly acquired friends at Duncroft, I did like the place. I was treated fairly, if strictly, and, unlike Columbine House in Norfolk, where I first entered the care system, and I and other children were regularly sexually groomed and abused by members of the staff and others, no one at Duncroft ever did anything similar. By the time the National Treasure turned up with his gifts of cigarettes, records and other stuff, I'd already formed a firm foundation of knowledge about what all men obviously wanted from females of any age, and so I wasn't in the least surprised by the 'favours' expected in return for the gifts.

Chapter Seven

Location: Court 13, Royal Courts of Justice, Strand, London

Timeline: 17 June 2015 – day three of the case

permanent: *adjective*: 'Lasting; remaining unchanged indefinitely.'

damage: *noun*: 'Injury or harm that reduces value or usefulness.'

It was my turn to 'take the stand'. I felt determined not to make an enormous amount of fuss or draw attention to my own weaknesses or ill health. The only possible clues to my being in anything other than rude good health were my walking cane, which I needed to maintain balance, and my inhaler which I kept on the table in front of me. The Claimant wasn't in court and I wondered if his legal team had advised him to stay away in case he got angry or frustrated; I quickly dismissed the notion as extremely unlikely and turned my attention to looking around the courtroom from a different viewpoint.

I tried to keep my face expressionless as my glance fell first on Helen, who had Peter seated to her left and Yinka, fussing over files and papers on her right and then, behind them,

David, who wore an intense but unreadable expression as he sat waiting for the clerk of the court to indicate the judge was ready to enter. Adjacent to David, the Claimant's team were busy preparing to begin their questioning of me. I noticed Susan seated on the benches at the back of the court; evidently, she intended to see how the rest of the trial progressed. I saw a couple of other people seated in the benches directly behind David, one of whom looked, to me, like some kind of legal representative, but who he might be representing I had no idea.

At hearing the now familiar phrase 'all stand' I had that weird sensation in my abdomen that my stomach or general innards had rolled over and over as I rose to my feet. I took it to be nothing more than a physical response to my emotional state, which was 'here we go'.

No way would my promise to speak truly be any stronger, or anything I said be more truthful, for my hand resting upon a Bible, or any other holy book for that matter. As a staunch anti-religionist (others would probably name me 'atheist'), I strongly felt that no good could possibly come from the involvement of an invisible, omnipotent being in all of this. I made my affirmation, desperately trying to keep my mind on the matter in hand and not let my thoughts wander off on a tangent, muttering to themselves about the idiocy of human belief systems.

Mr Dunham, the Claimant's legal brief, stood and regarded me for a few seconds. He then looked down at the lectern upon which he had several files and notes. A delaying tactic, I thought, designed to make me feel uncomfortable or even frightened. When he finally began to speak, perhaps aware that I was not in the least intimidated, he asked me about my early life and general childhood. Of course, I didn't have to give the court any of the gruesome details, but I admitted that my life as a young child and then later, as a teenager, had been far from happy or secure.

He asked me about how I came to be at Duncroft and I explained that I'd run away from my former care home in Norfolk several times. When asked, I was unable to tell him why other girls were at Duncroft and had to admit that even if I'd previously known why others were there, I'd since forgotten. Mr Dunham asked me if forgetfulness about the time I spent at Duncroft might have been due to the drugs I was taking. I thought he'd made it sound as if I were some kind of drug addict, so I answered that the resident psychiatrist had prescribed lithium, although I had no diagnosis of schizophrenia or anything similar. He spent some time asking how the lithium made me feel and I had to admit that it caused me to feel dizzy, groggy, faintly nauseated and affected my ability to do many things, including remember effectively. The point was further pressed when Mr Dunham asked if it were true that I could actually remember next to nothing about Duncroft. I replied that I thought I'd forgotten an awful lot more than I recalled and that it was probably a good thing. I'm pretty certain that wasn't what he'd hoped I'd say, but he didn't press the point at that time.

Directed to one of the large binders on my right, Mr Dunham then asked me to find a certain section and page number. I found a copy of a blog excerpt I'd made some years previously. It was entitled 'Being Full of Shit', which meant it had been blogged prior to my bowel cancer diagnosis, back when I spent the vast majority of every day sitting on the toilet. Mr Dunham drew my attention to a couple of sentences quite near the beginning of the entry in which I'd described myself as a 'drama-queen' and as having an innate ability to make huge mountains out of life's little molehills. As I scanned the page I recalled very well what this particular entry had been about, but the subject of the blog was not at all what Mr Dunham wished to discuss. He asked had I written that blog and I agreed that I had. He asked if the manner in which I described myself in that first paragraph would be, in my opinion, an accurate description. I readily agreed that it was an honest self-assessment and that I often did let things blow up out of all proportion. As soon as I'd seen what was on the page, it had been clear to me that Mr Dunham intended to make an attempt to somehow entrap me within my own written words, and so I hadn't been in the least surprised by his line of questioning. From the corner of my eye I could see Judge Nicol reading from his own bundle and, in fact, when Mr Dunham attempted to continue with his questions, the judge actually asked him to wait whilst he read the whole article. The 'writer's vanity', the very thing that had got me into the whole damnable situation in the first place, meant I couldn't help but wonder whether my writing had drawn the judge's attention although, with hindsight, I can see he was probably attempting to evaluate whether the words I'd written could be taken less as general self-descriptors and more in context to a particular incident.

Aware of Mr Dunham's irritation, I did my very best not to smirk or look smug, but it was difficult. Once the judge had finished his reading my cross-examination resumed and, it seemed, once again centred on the words of the blog because Mr Dunham kept going back to how I tended to exaggerate matters and react in ways disproportionate to the event in question. It was pretty obvious where this line of questioning might be leading, but I said nothing to deny the fact that I do have a tendency to overreact to many things which other people might think were unworthy even of notice, never mind reaction; not to do so would have been like trying to deny my own existence.

The morning had passed in the blink of an eye whilst I had been standing in the witness box. Just prior to rising for lunch, Judge Nicol addressed me and reminded me that I must not mention or speak of anything to do with the case, to anyone, not even my legal team. Peter once again escorted me from the premises and I stumbled, several times, as we crossed the busy road and joined the queue for lunch in Pret A Manger. Although I felt stiff and uncomfortably warm, the scarf once again sticking to my neck, the questioning had done nothing to diminish my appetite, for I felt ravenously hungry and quite content to ignore the case entirely whilst stuffing my face.

Peter and I were the first back to Court 13 after the lunch break; the clerk came to unlock the door in order for us to enter. I returned to the witness box and sat studying the woodwork from that viewpoint. I said to Peter that I didn't feel remotely intimidated, and therefore I must, surely, be retarded or something. When the clerk returned to the courtroom I spoke to her again of the beautiful woodwork and she seemed pleased to be able to impart a little more of her knowledge of the building, something she was evidently extremely proud of as well as her obvious pride in working in such a place.

All too soon the courtroom filled with people – including several nameless faces sitting in the back of the room from where they rudely stared at me intently – and then the judge returned, and matters resumed with Mr Dunham cross-examining me once more. This time, he focused almost exclusively on the evening in question and was most insistent that his client had neither tried to touch nor actually touched me. At first, Mr Dunham suggested I was 'mistaken' and then he implied that I was lying outright about the incident, although he didn't actually use the term 'liar'.

I found it increasingly difficult to maintain my aplomb because the righteous anger I'd developed had begun to boil and seethe inside. I must not be argumentative, I told myself over and over. It was hard, though, to endeavour to keep calm when I really wanted to scream at the blasted fellow. At one point, when Mr Dunham had strongly insisted the Claimant had not laid a finger on me that evening in 1974, I turned to the judge and asked, 'My Lord, may I speak freely?' The judge agreed that I could and so I explained that the Claimant had behaved in a manner that was entirely acceptable in 1974.

I added that he had 'goosed' me, and that this was something men of all ages did to women of all ages at the time. I had to further explain exactly what I meant by the phrase 'goosed' (because Mr Dunham claimed not to know what it meant). I told the court I'd lost count of how many times this had been done to me through my lifetime and that it wasn't this 'goosing' to which I had objected. I attempted to make quite sure that everyone in court would understand me by stating that, during the seventies, this kind of behaviour was both expected and accepted. I then added that I'd become distressed because, unfortunately, the Claimant smelled exactly the same as my stepfather, the man who had abused me throughout my childhood. My overwhelming need to escape and my tendency, even as a teenager, to overreact – not that I could have controlled my response, had I even tried – caused me to wave my arms frantically whilst crying out 'Don't touch me!' over and over again. At this point in my explanation, Mr Dunham interrupted and said something like, 'But he didn't actually touch you, did he?' I insisted he had done so and Mr Dunham insisted that I was mistaken or overwhelmed or hysterical. Whilst I had to agree that I might well have been both overwhelmed and hysterical I most certainly had not been mistaken. This line of questioning continued for some time and I think I failed somewhat in keeping my cool, because I knew I was replying to questions that felt like taunts in a defensive and argumentative manner.

Chapter Eight

Location: Chingford, London E4; Norwich, and various
other locations in Norfolk

Timeline: *circa* 1968–72

self-esteem: *noun*: 'A realistic respect for or favourable
impression of oneself; self-respect.'

The kids at the school in Chingford didn't like me any
more than had the kids at the school in Ludham. Although
not exactly shy, as such, I was nevertheless, quite withdrawn
and had little to no idea as to how to interact with people my
own age – or children of any age, in fact. Of course, there were
certain things about myself that I knew to be fact: I was ugly; I
was skinny; I was useless; I was stupidly thick… and all the rest
of the negatives drummed into me from the beginning of my
existence. Mostly, I knew I was different from the other kids in
some fundamental and indefinable way and, unfortunately for
me, all the other kids perceived this, too.

Life was nothing if not frightening and lonely in equal
measure. My home life brought nothing but sneering derision,
threats, constant blame for every little thing, not to mention

actual violence from Mother and, of course, once she'd gone off to work, the vileness of what I had to endure sexually and sometimes with violence from her rotten husband. At school nobody liked me or wanted to make friends with me. Teachers constantly berated me for not paying attention or getting things wrong and, when it came, inevitably, to lunchtime every day, the dinner ladies made my life hell because although I often felt really hungry I just could not eat the school food. I'd force my way through a little mashed potato and gravy or, now and again, perhaps some vegetables (so long as they weren't carrots), but I avoided the meat, which was seen as a terrible crime. Several times, after flatly refusing to put the meat into my mouth, I was slapped and sent to the head teacher for further punishment. Generally, this involved being called out the following morning during assembly and either being hit with a slipper or being given some other punishment such as missing breaks or writing out endless lines – all this enacted in front of the whole school. I'm perfectly certain I was called out far more than any other child in the whole establishment. Actually, the slipper didn't hurt much at all, definitely not half as much as Mother's big hands did, anyhow.

Sometimes, after school, I'd be 'sent outside to play', which actually would be more accurately described by the phrase 'sent outside for the other kids to tease, taunt, bully and laugh at'. I cannot recall how it came about that the local kids learned about my intense fear of water going over my head or into my face, but they lost no opportunity to lie in wait for me at corners of garden fences and hurl a bucket or bowl full of icy cold water into my face or over my head. Once or twice I was pinned into a corner by a group of kids bearing variously a hose, large water pistols and buckets of icy water. I shrieked and shook and wept and wet my knickers in fear, pleaded with them all to stop, to leave me be, but it never had any effect. They'd only leave me alone when something else more entertaining distracted them, and there were very few things more side-splittingly funny than watching the weird girl piss herself and cry like a little baby.

Mother had made a friend who had a daughter about the same age as me and I was often thrust into this unfortunate young girl's company. I can remember one day, very clearly, when I'd got mud on my white socks and moaned to the girl about how I'd get a hiding for it when I went indoors and she'd looked at me with wide-eyed disbelief. I learned then that she had never, ever been smacked or spanked in her entire life; this prompted my own disbelief and we almost fell out over it. The fact that she accompanied me to my home and actually heard Mother shout at me, saying she'd be giving me a good thrashing for the state of my socks, with her own ears was the only thing that stopped us from quarrelling. Even though that girl was extremely popular with the other kids she was never openly nasty towards me after that day, although she did try to avoid me whenever she could. Avoidance was impossible of course, what with our mothers having become such firm friends. I was invited to her damned birthday party. Never having been to a party in my life, I stood on the edge of little groups of excited girls at school talking about their special party dresses and matching shoes. Someone suddenly asked me about my party dress and I replied that I didn't have one. Of course, nobody believed that at all and I tearfully insisted I was telling the truth.

A few days before the party itself, I managed to utterly infuriate Mother, who had Nana with her and had told me to fetch something from her bedroom for her. When I arrived in the room, the most gorgeous yellow and silver party dress lay on her bed, its multi-layered net skirts lifting the yellow silky embroidered layer at least a foot high. Beside the dress were matching yellow and silver shoes, frilly knickers and little white socks. I looked at those garments longingly and thought how lucky my mother's friend's daughter was – it never crossed my mind that anything there would be meant for me; nobody would give such an ugly, stupid, horrible child such beautiful things to wear. I collected whatever I'd been sent for and returned to Mother and Nana – and to Mother's quite inexplicable rage. She simply couldn't believe I'd be so ungrateful and would not accept my breathless claim that I hadn't even considered the things were for me. I'm sure that, had she been able to get away with taking the clothing back to the shop and keeping me away from the party, she would have done just that.

As it happened, I was dressed up in the stuff and sent to the party anyhow – where every other little girl instantly became overtly jealous because mine was easily the most beautiful dress anyone had ever seen. But, of course, my appearing in it also proved to all the children that I was a complete liar, for hadn't I said I didn't own a party dress? Thoroughly upset by it all and never having been to a party before, I avoided all the games and felt too sick and tense to eat anything. Mother's friend thought I was maybe sickening for something, but in Mother's opinion I was doing nothing more than the usual trying to draw attention to myself. Once I got home and the dress had been safely packed away in tissue paper, I received the thrashing Mother thought I deserved for 'showing her up'. In addition to the violence, I endured the ever-present litany of how vile and awful I was in comparison to everyone else's children.

Nana simply could not understand how I had such a low opinion of myself. During the long school summer holiday of 1969, I found myself staying once more with my beloved maternal grandmother. That Mother and her foul husband had taken the baby off somewhere was simply a relief; I didn't express any curiosity as to where they might have gone and Nana obviously thought it strange – she tried to tell me, but I was way too self-absorbed and wouldn't listen. Eventually, I conceded that I didn't care because Mother and 'Daddy' didn't like me and I didn't like them either. I thought I'd be staying with Nana for ever because they simply didn't want me around. Although my grandmother showed some consternation about this and one or two other things I said, I don't believe she ever took me entirely seriously. Certainly, I'd never mentioned to her the horrible things 'Daddy' did to me every evening. I think I assumed she knew and, moreover, that it was perfectly normal and what everyone's daddy did. Although I did know, at least, one little girl who had never, ever been smacked and so, perhaps she'd never been assaulted or raped either, but I didn't know the adjectives to describe such events back then. Sadly, at only eleven years old, I hadn't made the connection that Nana had never, ever smacked me, or even threatened to do so, or that my suffering only occurred when with my parents and there were no other witnesses. I simply accepted that Nana alone loved me unconditionally, even though I knew I was absolutely horrible and worth less than nothing.

As a matter of fact, Mother had moved back to Norfolk, to Norwich, with her husband and little boy. Under the pretext of needing to completely gut out and redecorate the house they'd purchased, Nana kept me with her, although, when she finally took me to Norfolk to my new home, along with her brother and his wife (my great-aunt and great-uncle) with whom she would be spending the last week of August staying in a guest house in Sheringham, the room that was to be mine was still undecorated. I clung to Nana and begged to be permitted to go to Sheringham with her whilst tears flooded down my face and my breath caught in my throat, causing me to sob uncontrollably. Of course, Nana had to go and, just as soon as their car had pulled away, I unceremoniously received the first hiding I'd had for six weeks or so.

I hated the new house, all three storeys of it. It was a mid-terraced city house with nothing more than a nasty enclosed yard at the back instead of a proper garden, and a small paved area at the front only about four yards away from the main ring road. The air of the city smelled all wrong to me and the constant sound of traffic thundering past day and night made me fearful for the safety of our pet cats.

To my horror, during that first week Mother decorated the room allocated to me in pastel pink, of all colours, and so I hated that too, with a passion. Of course, I didn't dare utter a word about my dislike of the decor; it probably would've meant a thorough thrashing even worse than usual. Within the week I'd been kitted out in a new, rather posh and old-fashioned school uniform made of itchy maroon fabric with gold trim and then, one morning, Mother marched me along Thorpe Road to my new school – a fee-paying establishment – Thorpe House School for Girls.

Of course, I couldn't fit into that school environment either. For a start, I was different once again in that I never had tuck money or little personal things like a troll for the end of my pencil or pocket money for the tuck shop or pretty slides and ribbons for my hair. It took all of about twenty minutes for the other girls to notice such things; a few sneered openly and taunted me, saying my family were obviously poor and as such, I had no right to be there at their smart school. Mostly, though, girls avoided me – nothing new about that and I took it in my stride, finding things to do at playtime like peering closely at the rockery and ornamental bird feeders. When I asked Mother for money for school the next day she went absolutely nuts at me, raving and screaming obscenities. Although I quailed under the verbal onslaught I waited for her to draw breath before asking whether what the other girls had said to me was true or not, that we were poor. That earned me a really bad beating and

I had bruises for the rest of the week, not that they showed at school beneath the long tunic.

The top floor of the house was just one enormous room and, shortly after I'd moved to Norwich, Daddy started talking about using the room as a place to build a large train set. I tried not to show how enthusiastic I felt about that prospect, at least, not in front of Mother, but he kept drawing me into the conversations by asking if I thought I could make models, like trees, bridges and the like. Generally, I adored anything remotely creative, but I'd learned not to bring any of my creations home because Mother always made derisive, sneering remarks and threw them in the bin, usually after breaking them first so that I couldn't rescue anything. As Daddy enthused about the proposed train set, Mother folded her lips into a flat, disapproving line and actually sulked. Over the first few weeks of term the 'playroom' was fitted out with old rugs and some ancient, rather scruffy old armchairs that didn't fit anywhere else in the house and Daddy built an absolutely massive trestle-style table. Although Mother hadn't changed a bit whilst I'd been away staying with Nana, it seemed Daddy had. He even took me with him to the city-centre shops when he went to buy the first bits of the train set.

To Mother's evident fury I spent nearly all my free time up in the 'playroom' with Daddy even though she insisted I had to complete all my homework first. Daddy used to wink and nudge me. He'd whisper, 'hurry up' as he went past me on the way upstairs, his arms full of stuff for model making and scenery creation. It took very little time for me to completely forget how frightened I'd been of him back in Chingford; he became a sort of unofficial ally against Mother, quite often stepping between us when Mother flew into a rage and even, once or twice, shouting at her to leave me alone. By Christmas, the grooming was complete; if Daddy had told me to jump in the river because it would make Mummy cross, I'd have done it, even though I couldn't swim. That man actually cultivated the enmity between me and Mother with such deft expertise that I didn't even care if she noticed how deeply I detested her.

Whilst the train set was being built, Daddy was never anything other than nice to me. I spent many long hours carefully crafting pieces of scenery and buildings, painting papier-mâché landscapes and even making minuscule farm animals. Daddy began to set up the tracks; every week he bought a little more and every weekend, I watched as he added the new pieces. Together, we built a tunnel to go over a rather bare area of track, and then I made a farmhouse and barns to nestle in the valley beyond the structure. It was such enjoyable work and Daddy often praised me and told me how clever I was. When it was time for the train to make its maiden voyage I was so excited; I grinned madly as the little engine pulled its carriages around the winding tracks, through the tunnel, past the stations and goods yard I'd made. I was completely absorbed and delighted and totally not expecting to be attacked from behind and thoroughly, violently raped. When I screamed, Daddy was ready for that: he'd got one of Mother's silk scarves ready with which to gag me.

After that, every time Daddy told me to go up to the playroom to the train set I knew what it meant and, of course, I no longer wanted to go up there at all, not even when he bought me some new modelling supplies. Mother took obvious pleasure in sneering at me whilst telling me it was too late to change my mind now and other such things: serves you right; you're stuck with it now; that'll teach you... obviously by then she knew what Daddy was doing to me up in the attic room.

Mother constantly reminded me how disgusting, vile, useless, unworthy and utterly sluttish I was. She openly doted upon my little half-brother and actively prevented interaction between the two of us, so I turned to the cats for friendship and comfort. Try as she might, Mother could not influence the feline furries or make them dislike me, for they were not as easily dissuaded as her poor dog, always so desperate for Mother to be pleased with her that she would cringe away from me as soon as Mother made even a slight disapproving noise.

I seemed to fail at absolutely everything I attempted within a few weeks of moving to Norwich. My school marks suffered because I couldn't properly concentrate on anything; my mind would always be entirely filled with what might happen to me when I went home. I rarely completed homework satisfactorily. Mother would shout at me and force me to sit in the breakfast room at the table with my books, but at first, she didn't bother to look at what I was doing. Of course, once the school had contacted her to point out that I appeared to have fallen far behind the standard of everyone else in my school year and to express their concern at my withdrawn behaviour and lack of friends, that changed immediately: rather than simply shout at me to do the homework, Mother would loom over me and closely examine almost everything I did, none of which, in her view, was even close to satisfactory. She was ever generous with her sudden open-handed slaps if I didn't understand or couldn't get past the fear of doing something wrongly, so failed to do it at all.

One day, whilst sitting lonely and miserable on the rockery wall, a teacher approached and sat beside me. She was so chatty and friendly and seemed so open that I quickly responded to her. Over a period of around two or three weeks, I gradually told the woman what my life was like at home as well as pointing out that, if the other girls ever found out, they'd like me even less than they already did. The dutiful teacher went to the headmistress with what I'd told her and Mother was summoned and confronted. Even though she insisted I'd told hateful, terrible lies, she was forced to allow me to attend extra coaching in order that I could catch up academically as well as being referred to the Child Guidance Clinic.

In a desperate attempt to be accepted even a little, or at least no longer taunted as poverty-stricken, I began to creep downstairs late at night in order to enter the adult lounge to which I was never admitted. Having accidentally found a couple of sixpences and a half crown down the back of the scruffy settee in the sitting room, it seemed likely there'd be money down the back of the expensive furniture in the lounge. There always was, plenty of it too. When that source ran dry, I began to rummage through other girls' coat pockets in the cloakroom.

Of course, I was quickly caught and, much to Mother's fury, expelled immediately, as well as having my appointments with the psychiatrist at the Child Guidance Clinic doubled.

Doctor Stewart absolutely would not believe anything I told her. She believed what Mother told her though: apparently, I was violent and abusive toward my little brother, allegedly so eaten up with jealousy of him that I attacked him at every possible opportunity. Of course, this wasn't true and even though I vehemently denied it, my protests were simply regarded as yet more lies. When I told the psychiatrist about what Daddy did to me and had been doing to me since I was tiny, she didn't believe that either. She said it was 'preposterous' and I was sent off to a convent boarding school in order to curtail my 'inappropriate sexual fantasies about my stepfather'.

Actually, being away from home was the perfect answer with regard to both the things Daddy did and Mother's constant haranguing and violence towards me. Even so, I was hardly surprised by the realisation that, yet again, I really did not fit in at all. Not only had I never been to church in my entire life, but I also wasn't at all sure I could believe in an invisible being. Mostly, the nuns were kindly and, even the really fierce one – Sister Mathilda – was the one you'd run to if you had problems. Sadly, that particular diminutive little nun also taught mathematics and physics and found my obtuseness particularly irritating. In every other subject I did pretty well; it's not hard to succeed when one has such excellent teachers and mentors. Although I didn't exactly make any true friends,

I did manage to rub along with the other girls reasonably well, even though I often felt ignorant, outclassed and confused. I'd always feel particularly mortified when Mother came to the school for any reason because she put on airs and graces and was so clearly out of her comfort zone, having nowhere near equal status to the other parents.

In fact, the only periods of abject misery I experienced whilst a pupil at All Hallows were the holidays when I was forced to go home. Both my despicable parents resumed all former activities as if I'd never gone; how I managed to survive some of the thrashings I received, never mind the constant sexual assaults and rape I endured, I'll never know. After a particularly unpleasant half-term, I told the priest, in the confessional, what regularly went on at home and why I always tried to find an excuse to remain at the school during the holiday periods. He didn't disbelieve me; he was, I think, the first person to listen to me properly. He begged me for leave to break the rules of the confessional and allow him to go to the Bishop with what I'd told him. I couldn't risk that because I knew how clever Mother was at turning things about and anyhow, hadn't I been referred to the school by a psychiatrist at the Child Guidance Clinic? Father Godwin told me I could always come to talk with him any time I needed to, something I truly appreciated. Unfortunately, shortly after that, I was expelled because I slapped a girl's face. She'd actually been very unpleasant about Mother and said some unforgivable things and, whilst I loathed my parent, as far as I was concerned, I was the only one who should be publicly ridiculing her – and if not me, then no one else should do so. Violence begets violence, and physical attacks on me throughout my life had only taught me that this was the way to deal with difficult situations.

Chapter Nine

Location: Court 13, Royal Courts of Justice, Strand, London,
and inside my own head

Timeline: 17 June 2015 – day three of the case

truth: *noun*: 'The true or actual state of a matter.'
trauma: *noun (psychiatry)*: 'An experience that produces
psychological injury or pain.'

'Did you write these words?'

I stared down at a partial page copy of the first draft of my memoir which had been printed off from the website FanStory.com. I definitely had written those words, even though, before I'd self-published the book, I'd changed them a bit. I had to agree that I had indeed written them.

Mr Dunham schooled his expression before he asserted that, in fact, what I'd written was not strictly true. I so wanted to shriek at him, but instead I swallowed my irritation and politely disagreed.

'So,' he added, 'you're saying that what you wrote there is the truth?'

I agreed, yes it was.

Mr Dunham pointed out that within the written passage,

I'd stated that his client stank of booze and old sweat, amongst other things. I agreed that I had indeed written that; it was how I recalled events. Immediately, Mr Dunham pointed out that his client does not drink alcohol and never has done. He challenged me to comment upon that fact. What could I say? There would be no point whatever in arguing with the man; in any event, how was I to know what the Claimant did and didn't do back then – or even now, for that matter. I tried to describe the smell but words are not adequate to describe something as ephemeral as a scent experienced more than forty years previously. This was so incredibly difficult, I thought. How on earth was I meant to convey that particular smell? I didn't actually know the components that made up the odour, only that, even now, sometimes a man might pass me in the street, say, and 'that smell' will be upon him. The arrival of that particular combination of microscopic chemicals on my personal olfactory receptors has a very unpleasant effect, hot-wired as they are to that part of my brain I generally try to forget about: in short, that smell causes an instant panic attack. I tried to articulate this, but I think I actually only achieved further confusion.

Mr Dunham asked if I often panicked. I had to admit that I did, although perhaps a little less more recently than I had done in previous years. He added a query as to whether or not I perceived things as being more threatening than they actually were. How could I answer that? Panic is just panic and it doesn't have any kind of countdown criteria before it hits and so it would be impossible to say whether or not things were more or less threatening. I tried to explain that, quite often, I am not even aware of the trigger which causes the panic attack. Unfortunately, judging by the expression on Mr Dunham's face, I'd just managed to make myself look even more foolish. He went on to ask me about rather a lot of small, apparently insignificant, things relating to Duncroft, many of which I found myself entirely unable to answer because I simply could not remember. It was perfectly apparent, even to me, that Mr Dunham intended to show my memory as being particularly unreliable and there was absolutely nothing I could do about it. He touched again on the 'drugs', which had (according to my own written words, as he kindly pointed out) caused me to feel disorientated, 'foggy' and dizzy. In fact, that sensation, so similar to nausea and the general feeling of malaise, was what I could recall with incredible clarity because I so feared being ill, particularly in regard to nausea, with or without vomiting.

My mind wandered briefly and, in a detached manner, I looked subjectively at everything I feared in life: nausea; vomiting; loss of self-control; pain; anything which might precipitate any of the foregoing. When, I wondered, had the list become so short and concise? On reflection, perhaps it had always been that way; perhaps I'd simply needed advanced years and accumulated existential and observational wisdom in order to perceive it? It certainly explained why I had no fear of the court proceedings. Notwithstanding any other outcome to this case than my being utterly discredited and shown to be what Mother had always claimed, a troublemaker, I really had nothing to fear. As far as I was concerned, the whole thing was a complete waste of time, money and effort and the conclusion already set in stone. It would save such a lot of... everything if the judge just told everyone to pack up and go home, because it was plain that everything I'd said about anything was nothing more than my attempt to cause pain and trouble to everyone else.

Mr Dunham had asked me another question. Something about what I'd been wearing on the night in question. Of course, now the whole court needed to hear how I had been forced to dress in frumpy, old-fashioned clothing. I'd not actually been able to recall what I'd worn until Channel 4 News had managed to somehow unearth footage from the *Clunk Click* programme that showed me sitting directly adjacent to the Claimant. As soon as I'd seen it, I'd cringed; no wonder people had mercilessly taken the mickey out of me! The bright yellow blouse was baggy and unflattering, not to mention old-fashioned. The tartan skirt, the hem of which fell well below my knees but not as far as my ankles, made the blouse look even worse. If one covered my face and looked at just the body wearing the dreadful clothes, one would assume the wearer to be, at the very least, post-menopausal, if not entirely decrepit. In fact, when the picture had been shown on television a few of my current acquaintances had made comments which had been less than complimentary about my choice of attire – like I'd actually had a choice, I thought.

It seemed Mr Dunham now wished to speak not about my terrible clothing but another interview I had given, this one to the *Shropshire Star* newspaper. I recalled vividly how I'd told

Peter I'd give just one newspaper interview and that the first to call would be the one to get it. The *Shropshire Star* reporter had been a local man and the interview had been fairly brief; I'd had nothing to add to what I'd already said on film, which had been shown all over the news on about four different channels. I'm not certain if the reporter had been disappointed but, from what I could recall, he had not shown any sign of such feelings.

It would seem that, within the newspaper report, I'd said something about a celebrity who'd stuffed their hand up my jumper and then humiliated me. In all honesty, I couldn't remember ever having said such a thing. After all, I'd not been able to recall, at that stage, what I'd been wearing when the Claimant had humiliated me. I also couldn't recall any other celebrities humiliating, or for that matter, groping me or causing any distress. I had an inkling Mr Dunham knew full well that the printed words had been those of the reporter who had quite probably made certain assumptions when I'd said in the interview that a famous person had 'goosed' me and then made an extremely humiliating remark. Although my thought processes were reasonably clear, I could not account for the contents of the newspaper report. I knew I hadn't said that the Claimant had put his hand up my jumper, but, Mr Dunham reasoned that if it was in the paper, particularly within quotation marks, I must have said it. He quickly and expertly tied me up in knots with my own replies… and I let him do it because, deep down inside, I'd already given up and conceded defeat.

Suddenly, I felt so desperately tired, of everything – of being alive; of being here in court; of being in London; and all at such a great expense and a further debt I'd need to repay to Peter who had funded fares, accommodation, food, everything – since I had no resources. More than anything, I thought, it would be such an infinite relief if I could step out of my body and fade away into total nothingness. It felt to me as if I'd spent my entire life pitching myself, body, heart and soul, into one battle after another, and not by any choice or preference, merely in order to survive; there could be no respite. Many times throughout my lifetime I'd wondered if I was simply unlucky or whether, as Mother seemed to think, I'd deserved absolutely everything that had happened to me. It was all very well to fear loss of self-control, but I'd rarely, if ever, had control of external factors and I'd always felt as if life kind of dragged me along, willing or not, much like a piece of igneous rock being pulled over a landscape by a glacier; like a stray rock leaving grooves in the landscape beneath it, I'd left striations in the life history behind me, enigmatic signs that I'd passed through but nothing more. And what would happen when the metaphorical glacier melted or retreated, as is the way of such things? Would I be eroded and diminished, left entirely alone and unregarded in unfamiliar territory – much as a glacial erratic can be left stranded in the centre of a field surrounded by cliffs of sandstone as far from its origins as possible? I rolled this analogy around my thoughts as Mr Dunham flipped through his bundle.

He came to the part he'd been looking for and directed me to find it, giving me file, section number and page numbers. Once I'd found what he wished to draw my attention to, my heart sank still further: again taken from the FanStory website (without my knowledge or permission), was the rough outline of my life I'd jotted down in bullet points some years previously when I'd thought I would actually die of the bowel cancer with which I'd been diagnosed. Of course, Mr Dunham immediately drew my attention to the bullet point that stated I'd been handed down a twelve-month sentence of imprisonment when I was twenty. He read the bullet point out to the court and then, almost smirking, he asked if I had written the pages from which he'd quoted. I agreed that I most certainly had. I thought I detected a touch of malice in his tone as he asked me to confirm whether the statement was true. I had no alternative but to agree that, yes, it was indeed true. With a triumphant expression on his face, Mr Dunham glanced around at the occupants of the court before asking me, quite pointedly, to give the name of the crime for which I received the sentence. I replied that I'd issued cheques when there were no funds in the bank to cover them, which was classed as Criminal Deception. He made no comment about the severity of the sentence as compared with the 'crime', but it wouldn't have mattered if he had; he had effectively shown, again from my own written words, that, not only was my memory distinctly suspect, but I was also dishonest enough to have been required to be incarcerated at the expense of Her Majesty's Government.

I glanced across at the two reporters, both busy scribbling in their notepads. With mounting annoyance, I realised that here was another piece of my life which would likely be splattered all over the newspapers. Was there no end to all this? So much for having served my time and all that rubbish; even though the conviction had been thirty-seven years ago it would always be there for as long as I lived. I'd learned my lesson well enough; never again would I issue a cheque before there were funds in the account with which to honour it immediately. In fact, I'd sincerely doubt, even now, any ordinary person would be aware that to issue cheques when the funds are not available is a criminal offence; surely, everybody does it? I had to mentally shake myself free of such ungracious and doom-laden thoughts because Mr Dunham, having proved me dishonest by my own admission, had moved on to cast yet more doubt upon anything and everything I'd ever said or done.

During the course of the next hour or so, with occasional prompts from his team, Mr Dunham swiftly and expertly pulled me to tatters, just as the Claimant had told the live audience at his Wolverhampton gig back in October of 2012 he would. I did my utmost to maintain decorum and to be as brief and honest as possible but, by the time the cross-examination finally ended with the words 'No further questions, m'lord', I actually felt as if I'd been physically assaulted as well as psychologically and emotionally put through the wringer. My knees threatened to give way, and I actually considered 'letting go' of the hold I'd maintained on myself, but as quickly dismissed the notion. I did not want any newspaper to report that I'd collapsed in the witness box, which they would surely do. I did, however, stare at the floor beneath my feet and wish, most fervently, that I could sink down into it until I had vanished from sight entirely.

The judge called a halt for the day and the courtroom

gradually emptied. I sat still for a few moments because I really did not feel confident of my legs being able to hold me up; already, they felt as if they weren't mine. Eventually, I managed to find my feet and dither my way out of the witness box, down to the front bench to stand next to Peter and Helen. Peter squeezed my hand and whispered, 'Well done'.

Together, David, Helen, Peter and I exited the court and took the back stairs down to the entrance. I half expected there to be dozens of reporters outside but, to my intense relief, there were no more than usual and none of them took any notice of me at all. We crossed the road and went up Fleet Street to David's offices where he led us 'down to the bunker' (which turned out to be a recently decorated room in the basement) where we sat together around a table for a thorough debriefing. David said he was pleased with the way I'd conducted myself and that, far from looking like a criminal or someone who had made the whole thing up, in his opinion I'd come across as absolutely genuine. I tried for a cheerful, relieved attitude but I'm pretty sure it didn't work. I felt so very weary and could really focus on nothing much more than the prospect of a hot cup of tea and not needing to engage my mind in anything more complex than eating or drinking. At last, Peter and I bade David and Helen farewell until the morrow and left the offices. We were fortunate enough to find a black cab immediately; Peter ushered me into it and I noticed the concern on his face as he sat down beside me. If I looked anything like I felt, it must have been like sitting next to someone resembling a limp and wrung-out old tea towel.

Chapter Ten

Location: village near North Walsham, Norfolk; Columbine House,
Norfolk; Haut de la Garenne, Jersey, CI; and Duncroft, Staines

Timeline: June 1971–*circa* May 1974

juvenile delinquent: *noun*: 'A minor who cannot be controlled
by parental authority and commits antisocial or criminal acts,
as vandalism or violence.'

Mother was so furious when I got myself expelled from
the convent boarding school and refused to even listen
to the reason why I had smacked another student in the face.
Evidently, it did not suit Mother very well having me around
again for most of the time; she never stopped shouting,
slapping, punching, kicking me and was forever threatening
me with dire consequences for the smallest misdemeanour.
I felt that if I even breathed too hard she'd find that cause to
thrash and punish me.

They'd moved house again, this time to a sprawling 'cottage'
in a rural village not far from North Walsham. There were three
rooms downstairs, not including the kitchen and bathroom;
Mother had one for her bedroom. Daddy had the largest
bedroom upstairs, right next to mine. Not having planned to

be in the position of having to live at home again, fear made me bad-tempered and intractable. The way Mother dressed me like an old woman of eighty ensured that every other child between the ages of about three and nineteen would point and laugh at me. Before long, having become the laughing stock of the whole area, I'd actually managed, somehow, to make a friend, albeit the 'school troublemaker' who quickly introduced me to the arts of shoplifting, skipping lessons, hitch-hiking and generally running wild.

According to Mother, they'd had no other choice but to sell up and move because of the shame I'd brought down on the family by getting expelled from Thorpe House School. My despicable parent lost no time at all in making new friends in the village, mostly close neighbours and, at one and the same time, managed to persuade everybody that I was practically the Devil incarnate. That didn't assist me in the tedious process of attempting to settle and make new friends and acquaintances at all, although being clothed like an elderly spinster made things a thousand times more difficult anyway. The local kids took great delight in teasing, taunting and even physically assaulting me. Mostly, I tried to fight back, but after a particularly nasty thumping from a couple of village girls which left me with a pair of black eyes, a split and swollen lip and torn clothing, I gave up self-defence as entirely futile. Mother of course added to my injuries by thrashing me until I couldn't stand up, her reasoning being that I'd deliberately shredded and destroyed my clothes in order to force her to have to waste more of her hard-earned money on replacing them. Once I could move again, she sent me to my room with sewing needles and thread and informed me that I'd have to repair everything because she absolutely would not be manipulated into spending by such a rotten brat.

As said, I managed to actually make one friend at the large secondary modern school I had to attend in North Walsham from the age of twelve. Her name was Charlotte, but she preferred to be called 'Charlie'. She was an outcast, similar to me in some ways although her background was different – her mother had died, leaving her father to do his best to work full-time and bring up his daughter. Charlie showed me how to get myself marked as present on the school register both in the mornings and the afternoons and then, rather than go to the allotted class, slip away quietly, exit the school and go into the town. She was an expert shoplifter and in no time purloined some very, very snazzy, up-to-date clothes for me. We whiled away the hours shoplifting, sitting in the park with some of Charlie's friends – most of whom were either dead drunk or out of their minds on drugs – or chatting up local young men in cafés and outside takeaway shops.

Sometimes, Charlie went off with men and returned a little later, her cheeks flushed, her eyes bright and her laughter a little too forced and brittle; she always had money to spend after these occasions, and sometimes she would purchase alcohol. I did try the booze once or twice, but not only could I not get a taste for it, once I'd imbibed more than one, I felt extremely dizzy and vaguely nauseous, a sensation I found absolutely terrifying and abhorrent. Charlie could not understand how

I disliked the effects of alcohol, but she took my refusals as fortunate in that it meant there would always be plenty of drink for her, and moreover, I would always be sober enough to haul her to relative safety, or at least shelter.

In short, along with Charlie, I ran almost totally wild. The only times I was completely stymied would be whenever Mother had gone off to wherever it was she went with such regularity. Then my stepfather took full advantage of her absence and did whatever he pleased with me. Since my brother spent so much time out with his many friends, 'Daddy' was rarely disturbed. In fact, Daddy suddenly began to take me along to the social club with him on Saturday evenings where he introduced me to some of his friends. Occasionally, he took both my brother and me out to funfairs, social clubs and to visit friends. One Saturday, he took me into Norwich with him and spent a small fortune on very fashionable clothes for me. I kept insisting that Mother wouldn't like the clothes and would be very angry. Daddy said some pretty nasty stuff about both Mother and her opinions and then added that I could hide my new belongings in his bedroom because Mother would never dream of entering that room.

He then took me around to his friend's house and left me there, saying he'd be back in a little while. He and his mate had a hurried and whispered conversation at the front door. I suspected nothing; after all, I'd met Trevor before and he'd been nothing but friendly towards me. It started with Trevor asking me to show him my new stuff, which I did, most eagerly. Of course, then he wanted me to try things on and show him how they looked. Happy to show off, I felt only mildly embarrassed about changing my clothes in his living room whilst he turned his back. I drank several glasses of cola without ever considering the soft drink might be laced with something else. When I began to feel giddy, nauseous (and thus, panicky) I thought I was actually ill. Trevor took quite a few photographs of me before I was sick; most of them of me wearing very, very short skirts and no underwear. At least he looked after me and treated me gently, seeing me through my panic. When his homely wife returned from wherever she'd been, she was also full of sympathy for me and sat beside me, holding my hand and chattering right up until Daddy came back to fetch me.

I never knew whether Mother called the social services and asked them to take me away or whether they just decided to anyway. Mother made no move to stop the two patronising and simpering women who were waiting for me at home when I returned from 'school' one day. In truth, I'd spent all day in the park smoking cigarettes that Charlie had supplied and screaming with laughter at the jokes told by her and her friends. Mother had 'found' my secret stash of clothes, so she'd evidently been into Daddy's bedroom after all. They were strewn across the table and chairs and Mother shrieked and shouted about how 'tarty' and 'common' the things were and flatly refused to believe Daddy had purchased them. In front of the social workers, she named me 'slut' about a dozen times. It was quite a relief to be put in the car and driven away from my permanently enraged parent, although I had no clue as to where I might be going. I don't think I really cared.

One of the social workers described Columbine House as a 'reception centre', adding that it was run by Norfolk County Council. The social workers handed me over to Mark, the resident housefather, together with nothing much more than what I stood up in and a hastily stuffed carrier bag of personal items and a few pairs of knickers. At first, I thought I'd done well and 'landed on my feet', as the saying goes. Mark's wife, Zoe, the resident housemother, took me out shopping and spent a fortune on clothing for me, all of which was fashionable and came from boutiques and chain stores for young women. Over the moon with my new acquisitions, I happily packed them all neatly away in the wardrobe and drawers of my allotted bedroom.

There were about half a dozen other teenagers, male and female, in residence, but also some very young children. I felt incredibly awkward meeting them all for the first time, probably because I was expecting to be disliked and ostracised. However, all of the other residents were, at the very least, as damaged as me, some of them very much more than me and, against all probability, right from the get-go all of us teens got along reasonably well. The younger children bemused me utterly as I'd never had any interaction with kids younger than myself (except for my half-brother, interaction which Mother had severely restricted and controlled). One particular little girl clambered up on to my lap where she made herself comfortable, and without any consideration that I might not like it, began playing with my hair and chattering non-stop. Her subject matter switched constantly, sometimes even within the same sentence. Within a few minutes, I found myself completely and thoroughly confused whilst wearing a series of tight plaits, some thick, some thin, sticking out of my head at various odd angles. Before I could decide what to do or say, the child announced that she liked me, removed herself from my knees and went to join in a game with some of the other youngsters.

Although the food was excellent, the rooms more than adequate, as were all the other facilities, including outings, sports, and things with which to entertain oneself within its doors, there was a darker side to Columbine House. However, always rather naive and with a tendency to be extremely obtuse, I didn't actually notice it for several weeks.

One of the staff, Alan, was very trendy-looking, with fashionably long hair and a full beard. I'm not entirely sure how old he was at the time, probably in his twenties. All the kids loved him; he laughed often, played readily, gave teenagers illicit cigarettes and, in the evenings, after we'd had our baths and returned downstairs to the playroom for supper in our nightwear, he always dried and brushed the girls' hair. I loved the way he stroked my neck and behind my ears with his fingertips; it gave me goose pimples all over and sometimes made me shiver. I was entirely unaware at first that these subtle caresses were not a normal part of hair drying; after all, nobody had ever dried my hair for me before.

Then, when Zoe dried my hair one night because Alan had rushed to comfort one of the girls who'd run from the room upset about something, I noticed the difference. Next time I encountered Alan I asked him outright why he did those things to me when drying my hair. He grinned and twinkled, gave me a brief hug and whispered something like 'because I really like you'. There was never any violence or shouting, no curses or threats. I was entirely willing and complicit as the soft caresses became more adventurous. Certainly, Alan didn't rush me.

However, his attentions ultimately proved to be troublesome because, it seemed, he also showered all the other girls (except Jilly, the rights to whom had been exclusively claimed by Joseph, Alan's younger brother) with similar attentions. Arguments broke out between us as one or another claimed they'd had sex with Alan and he preferred her to the others. All were resolved, but I can't now recall how. Alan and Joseph's mother, who appeared to have housekeeping duties, was as strict and unbending as her sons were not; I know I feared her but I cannot remember why.

Once a week, Mark held a 'house meeting' in his study. Only the teenagers had to attend this. Generally, he'd be playing some kind of current music (I first heard Simon & Garfunkel in that study) and we were all given our choice of drinks... some of us had hot chocolate and others had... other things. The subject matter was always sex and Mark had everyone speak about matters such as masturbation, copulation, methods of stimulation and so on. Zoe was always present in the meetings, although she never said much. She stuck up for me when I was unable to answer Mark's question in a meeting, which had been to share with the group what I did in order to 'pleasure myself'. I hadn't a clue what he meant and became extremely alarmed when he stood up and loomed over me while shouting that I shouldn't try to be funny.

*

For the first time in my entire life I was going away on holiday. I'd only ever been to stay with Nana before then, and I'd never been out of the country – although even now, I'm not sure the Channel Isles count as 'out of the country'. Getting to the island of Jersey involved an extremely long and uncomfortable journey by minibus, all the way to Weymouth, Dorset from the depths of Norfolk, followed by a torturous period on a car ferry. I was seasick all the way there even though the ocean was calm. Seasickness is terrible for anybody, but for someone who suffers from emetophobia, it is the absolute end of the world. I truly wanted to die and, before the holiday had even begun, I was fretting about having to endure the ferry trip home.

We were camping; between us kids, we had about half a dozen or so tents and the adults had two tents. I shared with Valerie and Karen and the very first day and night truly were the most fun I'd ever had in my life before. We ate food prepared over a campfire, and afterwards, Alan got his guitar out and we all joined in with singing under the magnificent display of the Milky Way spread like glittering butter over the pitch-dark sky. The following day we spent mostly on the beach at St Ouen's Bay just doing ordinary beach stuff. I revelled in the hot sunshine, enjoying the beach like a little child.

The second or possibly third day of our holiday involved a journey in the minibus. We were going visiting, we were told. First, to Mont Orgueil castle and then, later on, to 'another place' nearby which turned out to be a children's home or reception centre, much like Columbine House only much, much larger. Whilst we were there, milling about on the driveway, something stupendous happened. The door of the building opened and out stepped none other than Jimmy Savile – the famous bloke off the telly! He had a fat cigar clamped between his teeth and wore a rather tatty old tracksuit. He held his arms way above his head and I could see he clutched several bulging bags in his hands. Children of all ages clamoured around him as he crossed the driveway to a large lawned area where, amid many protests of 'Now then, now then, look out behind', he sat down on the grass. The children pressed as close as they could whilst he handed out sweets and other small gifts.

Within a few minutes, we were urged, by Mark, Zoe, Alan and Joseph to go over to meet the celebrity visitor and get some sweets for ourselves. I did say hello to Mr Savile and he winked as he handed me a paper bag full of sweets; there was a five-pound note in the bag too, which caused me to goggle in amazement. I wondered if Mr Savile had put money in all the bags, but I didn't say anything, just in case it had been some kind of freak accident. I pocketed the money and scoffed the sweets. The afternoon involved assorted activities and the noise level was intense. I don't recall Savile being around through most of the games we played, although he was certainly present at teatime, sitting at the high table with the other adults. His distinctive voice was easily discernible even above the noise level of around fifty kids chattering and squealing.

And that scene is where my memories suddenly and inexplicably become fractured and strange, as if I'm trying to peer through thick, frosted glass. There are brief snatches of absolute clarity as if the recall had moved inexplicably closer to the other side of the glass: my being locked inside a St Helier hotel room with a Frenchman who required me to perform fellatio upon him before he penetrated my body in every way possible, multiple times; the beach at St Brelade's Bay being covered all over with giant hornets and the pain I felt because I stood on one before the beach was evacuated; the hugely muscled boxer on the beach at St Ouen's Bay one night, who carried me into the sea until he was up to his chest in water and told me he would drop me and stand on my head if I didn't stop screaming. I stopped screaming; he raped me and left me alone in the dark on the beach. Other, fleeting and far less clear memories of various sex acts with faceless, nameless people... and other vague memories of feeling almost permanently nauseous, although also of never being short of cigarettes or money. The adults from Columbine House were either absent, turning a blind eye to teenage smoking, or complicit in the provision of cigarettes, alcohol and who knows what else.

After that holiday, I 'absconded' from Columbine House on many, many occasions. Short of locking all my clothing away, allowing me to wear only my nightdress without slippers, or confining me to a locked room within the house, there was no way to stop me from running away. Sometimes I ran alone, at other times I went with one or more of the other teenagers. The Channel Islands holiday had taught me one thing of which I could be absolutely certain: I need never go without money because I could always, always get money for sex. I didn't have to enjoy it, and indeed I never did; I'd kind of detach myself from my body and float away on pleasant thoughts of Nana or of her beautiful garden whilst the pervert who'd paid would get on with whatever foul thing he wished to do. I had no idea where I was going when they moved me. In actual fact, I'd plotted with a local Hell's Angel to escape the night before leaving Columbine House, but my plans were foiled. I was caught – he'd already been arrested and hauled off by the police – and I was driven away by a social worker.

I saw the sign when we arrived in Moor Lane, Staines. It read: 'Duncroft A Home Office Approved School for Intelligent but Emotionally Disturbed Girls'. I asked the social worker what 'approved school' meant and she laughed the label off, saying that the place had changed hands recently and was now known as a 'community home school'. All I really noticed was that there were bars on nearly all of the windows and the outside doors were, without exception, locked. Members of staff moved about the place wearing bunches of keys on a chain at their waists which jingled as they walked. So, Mother's prediction about my being destined to nothing more glorious in life than being imprisoned had occurred at the age of fourteen, before I was even an adult!

The strangest thing of all though, was that not very long after I arrived at Duncroft, who should come visiting but Mr Savile! On these occasions he brought with him gifts more suited to young women rather than those that little children would enjoy, although I was mindful of the money I'd found stuffed in with the sweets. These included the latest chart records, perfumes, make-up and cosmetics and hundreds and hundreds of cigarettes. We were allowed to smoke at Duncroft, but our cigarettes were severely rationed, not simply by the amount of pocket money paid by the county council and/or our parents, but also dependent upon which 'grade' one happened to be in. Grades depended upon good behaviour, something I was not at all good at achieving, and so I was always more than grateful for the nicotine-laden bounty given so generously by our famous guest.

Chapter Eleven

Location: at home in north Shropshire

Timeline: *circa* 2008–12

unintentional: *adjective*: 'Not deliberate. Without intent.'

I'm not entirely certain which straw it was that broke the camel's back. The trouble was that all my life long there had been so very many traumas and they always came thick and fast, without pause. Anyhow, in about June of 1998 something inside me just snapped and I completely fell apart without warning and, on that occasion, for the first time ever, even after a few days, I was entirely unable to gather up the pieces of myself and so I simply ceased to function. I could not eat; I could not sleep; I had become mortally afraid of everyone and everything. Unable to overcome the fear and panic, I crouched miserably in the corner of my own living room and shook, from head to toe, so very violently that it was impossible to even hold a cup still enough to sip from. My poor children had to very much fend for themselves, not to mention care for me.

It must have been terrifying for them too; their feisty, pretend-confident and apparently assertive parent had utterly vanished and been replaced with a gibbering, stammering wreck. My daughter did her level best to keep the household running, and actually did a fine job. I was simply too ill to even notice, never mind praise or support her.

Any doctor will tell you that the human body cannot sustain a panic state for more than about thirty minutes; I found this to be quite true. However, what the body can do (and mine did) is to sustain a panic attack for thirty minutes or so, fall back to a short period of relative 'not-panicking' for around ten minutes and then re-launch into yet another full-blown panic attack. When this situation continues around the clock, for days and then weeks, it's time to summon help, and my daughter did just that. The doctor attended me at home and his visit lasted nearly two hours. He said that, in his thirty-plus years of general practice, he'd never seen such an acute and extreme breakdown, but he also reassured me that he could fix me.

At first, I simply had medication to get me through the acute stages – panic attacks and so on – and then, I was placed on a waiting list to receive mental-health services. Whilst waiting I became completely phobic about leaving the house – the very thought of going outside, even into the garden, filled me with abject terror. Several months passed and then finally, in the new year of 1999, I was given an appointment to see a psychologist. They even sent a mental-health support worker to fetch me!

Of course, the very first thing any mental-health professional would need to do would be to have a look at my antecedents and see what was likely to have triggered such an absolute failure within me. After three visits, when I still hadn't managed to tell her everything, Doctor McQueen suggested I write it all down: all my pains, disasters, traumas and troubles, everything I carried with me throughout life. She suggested, at first, just in bullet points, in chronological order as well as I could recall. I told her I'd always enjoyed writing in any event and so would produce the required document in time for our meeting the following week. This particular appointment was therefore more productive and some little headway was achieved.

The following week, I arrived at my appointment with twelve sheets of paper, covered on both sides with handwritten bullet points. I sat in a comfortable armchair and drank tea whilst Dr McQueen and her assistant, a CPN (community psychiatric nurse) named Ann, read through what I'd brought to them. When Dr McQueen finally raised her head, I couldn't mistake the deep consternation in her expression. I wondered if she'd begin with the same empty platitudes I'd heard a billion times before, or remark upon my 'vivid imagination' as had also been the case previously when professionals had discovered a tenth of what she now knew, but she did no such thing. She shook her head as if dislodging a heavy cowl, and her expression changed to one of unconcealed admiration. She said something like 'and it's taken all these years for you to finally stumble over and need help getting up. Amazing. You're so resilient. You should write a book.' I remember feeling embarrassed (I've never known how to accept praise) and making some sort of derisive comment about nobody wanting to read that kind of book, only to be astonished when both Dr McQueen and Ann averred, 'I would!'

I continued my appointments with the psychologist once a week for well over two years. By that time, many of my neuroses and panicky states were more or less controlled but I did have some physical ailments that simply wouldn't go away, despite the doctors at the GP surgery insisting the problems were all in my mind. The doctor who had attended me at the start of the breakdown had retired by that time and I didn't press matters; it was far easier to accept that my own mind was making me unwell.

I hadn't begun writing at that time. Dr McQueen had warned me that writing about my life would likely cause a recurrence of at least some of my symptoms, although at the same time be cathartic insofar as healing was concerned. I only actually began to write it all down in around 2005 when I had a reasonably decent computer to work with. The psychologist had been correct: writing it all down meant that I experienced things all over again, at least the emotions and fears if not the actual abuse. In fact, very little time was spent sitting at the computer at first because I'd rattle some event out, the words just falling off my fingertips and the act of typing apparently nothing to do with me, and then, with terrifying suddenness, I'd be overcome with all manner of things: rage, fear, confusion, pain and many, many more emotions and sensations. I'd weep, stamp about the room, shout at the empty air, sit down again, rise, pace about chain-smoking and sit again, drink endless cups of tea and coffee and continue to chain-smoke as my mind began the incredibly challenging task of facing up to the past, step by frightening step. In attempting to write down what had happened to me I had to confront it all again head-on and, even if I could not personally fathom why people behaved as they did towards me, most especially Mother, and particularly when I was very, very small, I had to deal with each event, no matter how small.

After a few months I began to notice a pattern emerging: I'd become entrenched in the disciplines of a writer almost without effort in that every day, after breakfast and seeing the kids off to school, I'd seat myself in front of the 'word-machine' with a large cup of tea and a supply of cigarettes and set to work. Although I'd slipped into writer's disciplines, I felt pretty certain that most writers didn't intersperse each chapter with foot-stamping tantrums or periods of bitter weeping and pain. Although writing it caused me intense distress, and probably, if I'm honest, did little for my kids, Dr McQueen had been perfectly correct: writing it all down was actually an excellent way in which to heal. I used the analogy, when speaking to the new psychologist, Dr Goodwin, that it felt as if the computer itself had taken all the crap I'd poured out of myself, like a giant tank or holding system. Whilst I could recall things still, they no longer bore the same sting that had originally hurt me so badly.

Mental-health services continued to encourage me and I continued to write. However, by 2006, I had discovered a writer's website, FanStory.com. For a small monthly member's fee, one could post things on the site and other members would read the posts and comment on them. These were not simply remarks about the content of the post (although there were plenty of those too). The vast majority were pointers about writing styles, identification of typos and poor grammar, spelling errors and even in some cases, information about rules of grammar and writing prose. Most of the readers, probably around ninety per cent, were American – the site was based in the USA, after all – and they very quickly got to know my little foibles and the 'English' spelling of many words. Part of the membership agreement was, of course, that I would read other people's work and comment in my turn. Reading is an excellent healing process in itself and I quickly found writers to whom I gravitated regularly because their poetry or prose lifted or touched me deeply.

The site had such an all-round positive effect on me that my healing gathered pace as did my writing. Five thousand words rapidly became fifty thousand and then two hundred and fifty thousand, and still I had barely even scratched the surface of the lifelong traumas. In fact, after winning a rather impressive trophy for being the site's fifth-ranked novelist during 2009, I decided to bring that particular volume to a close and begin a second. This volume began where the other left off, namely the very day that I first arrived at Duncroft, the Home Office Approved School for Intelligent but Emotionally Disturbed Girls. I continued to write, just as before, and within the first few chapters I'd recounted events involving Jimmy Savile, although at that point, since the old goat was still living and I was in mortal fear of him suing me (or worse), I used only the initials 'JS'.

One can always be wise with hindsight and now, looking back upon those writings, had I even considered that I had unknown British followers on that site, or even been aware that anybody, member or not, could read what was placed on the site (one only needed to become a member in order to comment and/or post up one's own writing), never mind print it off or download it to their own computer, I might not have used those particular initials in my description but rather 'X' or 'Z'. Of course, British readers would have immediately recognised the 'JS' as being Jimmy Savile, even had I used X or Y instead. He was always eminently recognisable from the simple description of his bleached blond hair, habit of wearing tracksuits, half a hundredweight of gold rings and neck-chains and of constantly smoking huge, smelly cigars.

Jimmy Savile didn't dress like a normal man. He always wore these nasty tracksuit affairs, made of some kind of synthetic silk that rustled as he moved. The trousers didn't have a zip; the waistline was elasticated meaning he could pull the trousers up or down quickly. Strange, on every occasion when I'd been obliged to masturbate or fellate him, he'd never been wearing any underpants. I wonder if he never wore them or simply removed them prior to taking me off for sexual activity? Nana's admonishment that one should always wear clean underwear every day, just in case anyone got to see, somehow, how terrible it would be if one was wearing dirty underpants!

Many people will dismiss what I say on this as being

nonsense and add that I must, surely, have been able to foresee that in writing this stuff down and posting it on a public site on the internet, it was almost certain to come to public attention. However, the simple truth is that it hadn't even entered my mind. Not only was I unaware of how easily anyone could read, download or print the story of my life and my experiences, I had little idea of just how many people might be doing this. In fact, had anybody asked me how many people I thought might be reading what I wrote, I'd have estimated it as well under a hundred, and those mostly from America. I'd never had much in the way of self-confidence, even though I was pretty good at pretending otherwise, and I really didn't think anyone at all would be interested in my life. Healing through the activity of writing, just as predicted by the mental-health professionals, was at the forefront of my mind.

Secondary to this, the very act of sitting at the computer and setting words down had reminded me that writing was something I really, really enjoyed doing. Although I doggedly continued to write about my miserable life, my imagination was rekindled and I also started to think about writing fiction. To that end, I wrote a few short stories that I posted on the FanStory site; these were well received and this encouraged me further. When somebody drew my attention to the annual NaNoWriMo contest (National Novel Writing Month; another American event) in which one is challenged to write a novel of at least fifty thousand words over a thirty-day period between first and thirtieth of November every year, my self-esteem had swelled just enough to consider that I might, possibly, be able to achieve such a thing. Using my youngest son as a sounding board and also enlisting Peter to bounce ideas back and forth with, I began, in around October of 2010, to thrash out the beginning, middle and end of a story I might write for this challenge I'd signed up for. There was no 'prize' as such, just a chance to get one's hands on a proof copy of one's story in paperback free of charge... dependent, of course, upon whether or not one achieved the challenge.

I set to with a will on 1 November 2010, and with little more than a vague storyline in my head along with a half-page of notes, my novel-writing challenge began to take shape. Actually, writing a novel in a month isn't that difficult; it works out to around one thousand six hundred and seventy words or so each day, which really isn't all that much, particularly not for me because I'd been chucking out at least five thousand words a day prior to that; even whilst writing the novel, I continued to add chapters of my life story to my folder on the FanStory site. My fictional novel had the unimaginative title *Hero's Tale* and was, actually, absolute and utter drivel, although as the possible bones of a future story or as a pilot story for a series, it held promise; nothing more. Even so, I was (justifiably, I think) extremely proud of my achievement of knocking out an actual book in just thirty days. I did as the NaNoWriMo site suggested and clicked the link to another site, CreateSpace, where my achievement could be set in print and bound and I'd receive a free-of-charge proof copy. More than anything, I wanted to hold the thing I'd written (however appalling) in my own two hands; apparently, this is normal.

CreateSpace contacted me several times to see if I was happy with the proof copy. Eventually, I signed into the site and agreed I was content with it and, shortly thereafter, it went on general sale on Amazon (CreateSpace is an Amazon company) in both the UK and America. Although it felt quite good to have something I'd written 'on sale' for anybody to buy, I'd already used CreateSpace to vanity publish the first, extremely long-winded, part of my life story – my biography, I suppose – and I was under no illusions. I knew that the chances of actually making any sales were pretty remote. I was unknown, both books I'd self-published went to publication unedited and unrevised and, in my heart of hearts, I knew both to be poorly written piles of unadulterated trash. Even so, at that point, I'd healed from most of my past traumas, if not completely then at least well enough to allow me to see that the biography writing, however long-winded and unnecessarily over-detailed, had indeed had a cathartic effect and was continuing to do so. The short novel had done nothing more fancy than boost my confidence (something I sorely needed because it had been at well below zero throughout most of my life). I now knew there was something I could do reasonably well, that I enjoyed and which held possibilities for positive steps in the future, although I also believed, realistically, I'd never be able to make my living at writing.

In any event, I just got on with writing my biography as before and posted each chapter up on FanStory.com. Once in a while, I entered various contests on the site, both for poetry and prose. In addition to that, I became fairly well recognised in that particular little community of writers. Some few writers added me as 'friend'. A couple of dozen followed my writings as 'fans' and I, in my turn, followed some of the writers whose work had particularly touched or impressed me. In fact, some of the friendships that grew out of the shared interest in writing led to me making further contact with some writers away from FanStory. On various other social-media sites, we were able to chat, exchange news, views and tips and even, on one site, play my favourite word game: Scrabble.

As I write, I would still consider at least fifteen people I first encountered through FanStory.com to be friends. I've met a couple of them – only the British, of course; I couldn't afford a flight to the USA or Australia – and I have one social-media friend coming from Australia this year (2016) to stay with me for a couple weeks. For probably the first time in my entire life, I suddenly found I had friends, in itself a novelty. I'd always encountered dreadful problems when endeavouring to make friends, and I seem to manage to lose them even more rapidly than I can make them. However, I'm not a completely friendless person…

I met Rosemary one night in 1979 when her husband Tom took pity on me because I was homeless at the time and so he took me home with him once I'd finished my shift behind the bar of the pub where I worked. After a first glance of undisguised horror at the sight of me, Rosemary remarked, matter-of-factly, that I was far too skinny and clearly in need of a good feed. To this end, she cooked a mountain of eggs and chips – this was well after midnight – and presented it to me on a tray with a pint mug of steaming hot tea. As I ate, we chatted; even once I'd finished eating we continued our conversation until the grey light of dawn filtered through the curtains. Fortunately, since it was a weekend, Rosemary didn't have to go to work. She made me up a comfortable bed on a pullout settee and I slept as if it was the finest bed money could buy. Although we look like chalk and cheese, after thirty-six years, Rosemary is still my best friend.

There is, without doubt, a great advantage in having friends, not least because one can share anxieties, thoughts, ideas and more, but also lend support when it is required. With my newfound friends, daily writing of my biography and continuing therapy from mental-health services, I believe I actually began to grow as a human being after having been stunted and deformed psychologically and emotionally by my childhood experiences. Sadly, as is often the way of things, just as my psyche began to function more normally and I discovered a joie de vivre I'd never even considered possible, so my body made its own plans and did something truly horrible.

Chapter Twelve

Location: Duncroft, Staines; BBC Theatre, Shepherds Bush;
and various other locations

Timeline: 1973–4

manipulate: *verb*: 'To manage or influence skilfully,
especially in an unfair manner.'

I liked Duncroft. Actually, that's a sweeping statement and it isn't exactly true, but it does suffice for anyone who doesn't need to know all the ins and outs and details. In fact, although I still managed to ostracise myself within my peer group, Duncroft was such a blessed relief, mainly because the adults in attendance were not abusers. Of course, being a teenage girl, I often found myself on the wrong side of the rules and in trouble to varying degrees, but that trouble never involved being assaulted, starved, raped, or any of the other things I'd suffered at the hands of Mother, stepfather and so-called caregivers. In general terms, punishments for most wrongdoings involved a temporary loss of certain privileges, such as being permitted fewer cigarettes, less time watching television or going out in groups to various places. Most of my misdemeanours were minor, but I did abscond a few times, usually because despite my best endeavours to avoid it, I was being sent home for a weekend or holiday period.

There were many household chores to be completed daily and, of course, with about two dozen girls in residence, plenty of young hands to undertake them. Much to my disgust I learned how to clean toilets, bathrooms, staircases, linoleum flooring, tiled flooring and much, much more. Members of staff only loosely supervised the work as it was being done, although they did check it once the tasks were 'finished'; it had to pass a certain level of scrutiny before we could rest awhile. There were also school lessons held in a separate building but, in all truth, these were very limited and quite basic. I did have to learn typing and shorthand, also much to my despair. I'd much rather have spent all my allotted academic hours writing essays, reading or dressmaking, and besides, Mother did shorthand and typing and in no way did I wish to resemble my nasty parent.

Whilst most of the other inmates either avoided me or openly taunted me, there were two or three girls with whom I managed to rub along without too many hitches; I counted them as friends but I'm not sure if they regarded me as such. Together, we played an awful lot of partner whist in the afternoons and early evenings.

Jimmy Savile arrived regularly at weekends, and sometimes visited during the week. Occasionally, he even stayed overnight, although in all honesty I cannot recall, with any clarity, much about that save that we all gossiped and speculated and giggled about his possible intentions towards Miss Jones, who overtly simpered and smirked whenever she was in his company. Of course, we'd also thoroughly gossiped about the possibility that Miss Jones was a practising lesbian prior to Jimmy Savile turning up. It's amazing what the minds of adolescent girls can come up with.

Even though a great many of us suffered at the old pervert's hands, we still giggled and sniggered about it all. I'm perfectly certain that not a one of us even considered that we were being abused; at least, I definitely didn't, if for no reason other than I'd not been beaten, plied with drugs or alcohol or forced in any way other than through the use of clever persuasion and manipulation. Whilst I actively disliked having to handle Savile's penis, fellate him or permit him to grope and fumble about at my unformed breasts and down my knickers, I did very much enjoy being taken out in his car either alone or with a group of others. When he vowed he would take me and some of my friends to the BBC in order to take part in his then show *Clunk Click* if only I would fellate him, I performed the vile act (almost) willingly. On the first occasion, I retched violently because he thrust his pelvis forward and then needed to lean across me to fling open the passenger door of the vehicle as he urged me, 'Not in the car! Not in the car!' However, that incident didn't appear to put him off in any way and he did keep his word, even though one of my 'friends' insisted I should have ensured I got the reward before performing the sexual favour.

I went to the set of *Clunk Click* on around five occasions, much to the annoyance of some of the other girls. The fact was, Jimmy Savile obviously liked me for some inexplicable reason and I was often amongst those he selected to go with him out in his car and to attend the shows. At the time I felt important and I rather revelled in my 'special' status, particularly since, on at least one occasion, I attended the show in London even though I'd been downgraded for some misdemeanour and was supposed to be grounded. It won me no friends at all, of course, but I was so used to being disliked I'd become fairly thick-skinned about it and considered the treats and privileges afforded to me by the delightful Jimmy Savile to be worth my being hated.

I'd also grown used to the constant comments about my appearance – how old-fashioned my clothing and footwear were and how frumpy and 'old' I always looked. Not old in the way a teenager wants to look older than her meagre years in order to drink in a bar or purchase adult goods, but old as in I was often forced to dress like an old woman. Mother's choice of clothing for me had long caused me such a lot of misery, so that by the time I arrived at Duncroft, even extremely cruel remarks had mostly lost their sting. Starry-eyed and thrilled with the prospect of both being on television and meeting so many famous people, I arrived at each show clutching my autograph book like a talisman. The book rapidly filled with signatures of well-known television, pop and film stars. Not everybody I met was any kind of closet pervert, although there were quite a number. Of those who shared Jimmy Savile's liking for underage sexual partners, most left me entirely alone, for which

I felt pathetically grateful. Gary Glitter, for example, made me want to vomit, but on the evening to which I referred in my memoirs, he had moved his attentions to another Duncroft girl who openly adored him, a fact he took full advantage of. At this point I should like to state, quite categorically, that at no time, to my knowledge, were the Claimant and Gary Glitter ever on the same show together, in the same room together or in any way linked to one another, despite what the papers said at the time the revelations came to light.

On the occasion when all this business with the Claimant began, I was present at the BBC Theatre in Shepherds Bush with five other Duncroft girls, one of whom was Susan Bunce. In fact, the Claimant was absolutely entranced by Susan. What man wouldn't be? As I've already mentioned, I secretly kind of hero-worshipped the girl myself, and so I could quite well see why the entertainer would be attracted to her. Having been seated pretty close to both Susan and the Claimant during the recording of the programme, I was aware that the latter smelled almost exactly like my stepfather. Susan didn't appear to notice. I suppose this 'odour' should be described as a 'man-scent' for, as I've already said, I have noticed it or personal body-smells so similar to it many times since that night and unfortunately, every time, I am flung backwards in time (without so much as a 'by your leave') into panic. In any event, the Claimant's focus of attention was mainly – but not exclusively – fastened on Susan for most of the evening.

Jimmy Savile himself dominated the 'dressing room' in which everybody gathered after the show had been recorded.

Still attired in his trademark tracksuit and dripping in gold chains, rings and bracelets, he sat on his throne-like chair, generally with a child or young person jouncing on his knee, holding court with his foul cigar smoke weaving through the air as he pontificated and laughed. He clearly revelled in his fame and fortune and certainly projected an aura of absolute rightness about the whole situation. Various lackeys, probably employed by the BBC under the label 'hospitality', drifted in and out of the room bearing all manner of delights. One plate, left on the end of a table, held the contents of about four packs of cigarettes, although why they were placed there I couldn't guess, unless it was solely in order for the Duncroft girls to help themselves. As a smoker surviving on extremely tight rations, any extra cigarettes were always more than welcome; virtually all the Duncroft girls smoked.

Savile himself made no secret of the manner in which he pawed at his young guests. One of his little foibles in fact was that he liked to sit a child on his knee, his hand resting on their lower back whilst he jiggled and bounced them around. Once he had become aroused, he would slip his hand down under the back of the waistband of trousers or skirt and fumble about in the victim's undergarments. He and his guests made endless sexist remarks and jokes – all of which was perfectly commonplace and acceptable behaviour from men at the time – and more than once I noticed the 'servants' smiling or laughing along with him. I don't believe anyone thought it remotely unusual behaviour for Savile or most of his guests; it was just 'show business'. Savile himself was virtually a god in the eyes of the nation and most of those around him; he was untouchable and many people thought him a saint – albeit a rather peculiar and eccentric one. His peers, famous persons from all walks of life, were almost as powerful, some even more. Mostly, they were beyond reproach and any complaints would have fallen on stony ground whoever the complainant had been; a child from an approved school would certainly never have considered such a thing.

Besides, as already mentioned, attitudes to women and girls during the seventies were shameful, although this was probably partly due to the 'revolution' of the sixties, when many young women had shaken off the shackles of what was considered 'proper', thoroughly shocking their parents and relatives by their actions. Psychedelia and flower-power notwithstanding, for men to grope and paw at women's bodies, even very young women – because there was never really any line drawn, however metaphorical, of where 'age-appropriate' or 'unacceptable' might lie – was just something that happened with monotonous regularity. I can vaguely recall occasional remarks being made by older men (relatives and strangers alike) to little girls of perhaps ten or eleven years old about the possibility of soon-to-appear-breasts and how they might be used to good effect when the girl wanted something! The facts of the matter were simple: everybody accepted this kind of behaviour and, if anybody minded, they didn't speak out about it.

The way I reacted to the Claimant's 'goose' drew a lot of extremely unwelcome attention, mainly in the form of laughter, from those gathered in the dressing room on the evening in question. For me, simply the scent of the man was enough to hurl me back in time to a place very definitely unsafe, frightening and full of foreboding. I don't believe anyone realised at the time that it hadn't so much been the actions of the entertainer that caused me to freak out, but something else entirely.

After the 'titless wonder' comment, he had moved off amongst the crowd, most of whom were laughing at my expense. Mortified, I'd have been so grateful had the floor opened up and swallowed me then and there. There were tears; of course there were tears. There were also a few well-chosen remarks from other Duncroft girls about my breastless figure.

After that show, on the return trip to Duncroft, there was a lot of laughter and apparently endless jokes and spiteful remarks about me, my lack of womanly curves, the way in which I reacted and how it had made me look even more ridiculous than usual. Another girl who had spoken of her embarrassment at the Claimant's offer of some of his pubic hair as a memento (described later in Chapter Twenty) had managed to recover somewhat in that she aired the opinion that the Claimant was, basically, a disgusting little man, which somehow made what had happened to me even more funny in the eyes of the other girls. Although I don't recall anyone saying or doing anything unpleasant to Susan, the chances are they did. I never could understand why mostly the other girls disliked her so much.

Once we arrived back, and the taunting and jokes didn't

cease, I severely 'lost it' and my foul, uncontrollable and vicious temper took hold. Entirely out of control, sickened, frightened, upset and aggrieved, I screamed and yelled, threw things about and did a fair job of wrecking the dorm I shared with three other girls.

A few days later, when obliged to go home for the weekend (much to my despair – as if I hadn't already dealt with enough that week), I told Mother and Nana about my visit to Shepherd's Bush in London for the filming of the *Clunk Click* show. Nana of course listened and then insisted we sit and watch the damned programme whilst Mother muttered darkly about the modern concept of rewarding horrible, bad, wicked children with treats, holidays, outings and the like that decent, good, honest children would never, ever have the opportunity to experience. I tried to explain to Mother that it wasn't actually within my power to control these matters but, of course, she wouldn't listen. Her outrage grew exponentially and, before the programme had even begun, she had clouted me several times for 'insolence'.

Once Mother saw me, sitting on a beanbag on the stage, rubbing shoulders with none other than the Claimant and, as she said, 'simpering and flirting in an outrageously disgraceful manner', she slapped me again, despite Nana's weak protests. My eyes streaming tears, not just from the stinging blows I'd received, I yelled at Mother and told her the Claimant was horrible, smelled like her foul husband and, after unsuccessfully goosing me, had called me a 'titless wonder' in front of everybody and that they'd all laughed at me. Nana shook her head sadly and did her level best to calm the situation, but Mother smirked nastily at me. Her ice-blue eyes glittered with malice as she retorted that the Claimant had told the simple truth: I was skinny and scrawny and utterly, completely 'titless'. A sob caught in my throat and more than anything in the world, right then I wanted to smash my horrible parent's face to a pulp. Seeing the expression on my face, Mother added to her nasty echo of the Claimant's observations that, in one regard, the entertainer had been totally wrong, for, she said, there was absolutely nothing whatever wondrous about me. Nana made some conciliatory remarks whilst I sobbed my way through the broadcast of the show that had caused me such distress. The rest of the weekend involved a great many similar incidents because Mother felt justifiably outraged that I should meet celebrities and go to theatres and performances, never mind my trip to Wimbledon the previous summer, which she'd never stopped complaining of, when I'd always been nothing but trouble, a waste of space, ugly, stupid, worthless and all the usual negative things she'd drummed into me lifelong. People like me, she averred, most certainly should not be rewarded, not ever.

Chapter Thirteen

Location: at home in Shropshire

Timeline: February–November 2011

deceive: *verb*: 'To mislead by a false appearance
or statement; delude.'
persuade: *verb*: 'To prevail upon a person to do something,
as by advising or urging.'

Whilst my psyche had certainly done most of the recovering it was ever likely to do, I remained pretty much disabled, but almost exclusively by physical problems. My body had, whilst I was busy getting my mind and ego fixed, sneaked up on me. In short, for over a year, I'd suffered dreadful, uncontrollable diarrhoea, which had prevented me from leaving the house. On the rare occasions when I had no choice but to go out anyway, I'd need to dose myself thoroughly with loperamide, wear maternity-style sanitary wear and carry spare underwear in order to do so. The kickback of that would always be, if the diarrhoea temporarily stopped, which it didn't always do, I would feel desperately sick, which caused even further problems. Emetophobia had controlled my entire life, and finding myself alone, out of the house and my 'comfort zone', as it were, with the unpleasant and terrifying possibility that I might vomit at any second, was an experience I needed to avoid at all costs. Even though my doctors obligingly prescribed regular anti-emetics for me, if the diarrhoea stopped through the use of drugs, the feeling of nausea and imminent eruption would be uncontrolled (although, in truth, I never actually vomited).

In late 2010, my doctors had just begun to come around to the idea that my bowel problems might not be of psychological origin after all, as I had frequently been told. Of course, ever contrary, the episodes of diarrhoea abruptly stopped at that point and so no further investigations were undertaken. I still felt sick most of the time though, but the medics were completely certain it was psychosomatic and so they continued to prescribe anti-emetics and I continued to take them.

In February of 2011, I experienced something entirely new to me: constipation. I'd never really given very much thought to the condition but, after more than a week of needing to 'go' and being unable to do so I began to feel rather concerned, especially since although my anti-emetic medication successfully stopped me from actually vomiting, it no longer stopped me from feeling nauseous. After a fortnight of feeling uncomfortably full, sporadic retching and subsequent panic attacks I decided I had no alternative but to visit the doctor; I recall feeling mightily miffed that there was no female doctor available for an emergency appointment.

Anyhow, I knew I needed to see a medic and so, taking my friend Caroline with me for moral support, I visited the surgery and spoke with Dr Smith. He listened carefully and then, of course, wanted to perform a rectal examination. Sadly, the one thing from my past which has never healed or lessened has been the abhorrence and panic I feel at the prospect of being intimately examined by any male; I refused. Dr Smith seemed to understand. He gave me a prescription for a laxative and told me to make an appointment to see one of the female doctors at my leisure. Within an hour of my visit to the surgery, and before I'd even had the opportunity to collect the prescription, nature took its course at last. Lulled into a sense of relief by this, my anxieties faded and I relaxed somewhat and got on with my writing. I had to 'go' several times, but this didn't particularly surprise me; after all, I hadn't 'been' for nearly a fortnight so there would be a lot to be rid of. However, when the passage of stool was abruptly replaced by the passage of a great deal of very bright red blood, I panicked completely, in fact, worse than that... I reverted to the breakdown state.

Peter came over and did all he could think of to help me, finally having to resort to summoning the doctor for a house call. The female doctor who attended me did more to allay my fears than anyone or anything else. She told me she'd book me in for an urgent colonoscopy and further reassured me that, unless I lost a large amount of blood on a daily basis, I'd come to no harm whilst waiting for the appointment.

Even as an urgent case I was obliged to wait until June of 2011 for the dreaded procedure. Whilst waiting I only experienced one more bleed and no further attacks of constipation and I convinced myself that the horrible procedure would discover irritable bowel syndrome or at worst, diverticulitis. I was much more worried about the possibility that the bowel preparation might cause me to vomit than about anything else but, with the support of my three sons and Peter, I got through that all right and Peter drove me to the hospital the following morning. The hospital staff were very kind and reassuring and the procedure went off without any trouble. I'd elected to be sedated but, much to my amazement, the sedative actually sharpened my senses rather than dulled them. I was sent to rest in recovery for a while and then dressed and sent into a sitting room where I was obliged to eat a sandwich and drink tea. By the time Peter and I were summoned into a small adjoining room to speak with a doctor, the sedative was doing what it should have done much earlier and I barely heard what the man said, and what little I heard passed over my head completely. The doctor handed me a sheaf of papers and said I was free to go home.

Much later, after I'd had a good sleep, Peter showed me the report and explained that the doctor had taken various samples to send off to the laboratory for testing. He didn't tell me what they might be testing for and it didn't occur to me to speculate, so when I received a phone call from a colorectal nurse just two days later, I resisted her plea for me to come to the hospital the very next day. Eventually I agreed to attend and after I'd hung up, sat and stared at the colonoscopy report that I held between trembling hands. I finally understood what had been found: amongst several polyps nestling in my lower colon and upper rectum, lurked a 'growth' of approximately ten centimetres in diameter, itself misshapen, oozing pus and blood – I had cancer.

A very strange reaction occurred within me once I realised

what was actually wrong. Rather than panic, as I may have been expected to do, I actually withdrew into myself and thought quite calmly, 'Well, that's that, then.' Peter came with me to the emergency hospital appointment and I sat in front of the doctor and calmly informed him that he wouldn't need to waste time or resources on me because I absolutely knew I couldn't go through the treatment for cancer or any surgery... because it would make me vomit and I feared vomiting far more than I feared cancer. Nevertheless, the poor fellow patiently explained what would happen next, although I didn't hear what he said. I drifted off into a strange, insular little world of my own where I began to plan making my will, arranging my own funeral and to worry about not having any material goods to leave for my offspring. Peter, being a fully qualified nurse, listened intently, asked pertinent questions and queried whether or not I might be given options. I let him get on with it; I felt it was nothing to do with me.

I told two of my three boys when I got home – the third was on holiday in Spain and we decided not to ruin his holiday by calling to let him know. The eldest son automatically assumed I'd be having treatment and spoke in a positive, supportive and encouraging way, promising that everyone would help me to fight the disease. However, the youngest, probably the one who knows me best, waited until we were alone before saying 'You're not going to take the treatment, are you?' Gradually, over the period of around a week, it occurred to me that dying from cancer wasn't as simple a thing as just giving up and refusing treatment. In fact, the more I learned about bowel cancer –

mainly from Macmillan and other internet resources, the more I discovered that I was extremely unusual in that I'd not yet vomited at all – probably more to do with the fact that I scoffed anti-emetic medication with monotonous regularity than for any other reason.

Peter accompanied me to the next hospital appointment to see the oncologist and I sat shivering with terror as he explained that there would be a 'three-pronged-attack' on my tumour: chemotherapy, radiotherapy and surgery. I told the fellow I didn't want the treatment and that I absolutely couldn't do anything that might make me vomit. Peter patiently explained my emetophobia and how it controlled my life, and of how the prospect of these three types of attack upon the disease was the worst possible thing that could happen to me. The oncologist had evidently heard similar before because he quickly explained that the chemotherapy drug they used for my type of cancer was administered orally and so would be actually be pretty useless if patients vomited it back up. I was assured that the treatment would be extremely unlikely to make me vomit but that refusing treatment meant I would become more and more unwell and, as the cancer spread about my body, vomiting would become a regular and painful problem.

Actually, I only had three days' worth of chemotherapy in the end because I had some rare reaction to the damned drug, which affected the function of my heart in an adverse manner. However, I went for radiotherapy every day for a six-week period, travelling fifty-five miles into Wales and fifty-five miles home again on each occasion. I'd been told that, once the radiotherapy sessions had been completed, I'd have a 'rest period' of about six weeks before surgery, which would leave me with a stoma (of which more in Chapter Sixteen). The concept of an abdominal stoma didn't trouble me, oh no. The only thing about the planned operation (other than it was not the one I would have elected to have, had I been given any say in the matter) that frightened me witless was my conviction that the anaesthesia would make me vomit.

I really needed that rest period for I had become painfully thin over the course of the treatment, and the diarrhoea had returned with a vengeance. I could no longer write or concentrate on anything much at all and had become so tired and weary I could barely function on any level for longer than about half an hour. Despite my doctors doing all they could to reassure me, I knew things didn't look too good by the way they were all urging me to try to improve my appetite and gain a little weight prior to surgery. In fact, by the time I reached the end of my radiotherapy sessions, I thought I knew, deep down, I would not survive the surgery and so, once more, I began to worry about what I would be leaving behind for my boys... nothing but debts, as things stood.

When, out of the blue, shortly after my treatment had ended, I received an email from CreateSpace informing me that they had been contacted by none other than the BBC in regard to my book *Hero's Tale*, a great surge of relief and gratitude flooded through me. The email implied that the BBC wished to make something from my story and this would obviously mean I'd be paid for my manuscript and ideas. Over the moon and with delighted optimism, I contacted the boys and let them know what had happened before I called the number passed on to me by CreateSpace. I found dialling the number difficult on account of my trembling fingers, but for once, the shaking and unsteadiness were the result of excitement and anticipation rather than panic and dread. The lady who answered my call sounded friendly and said she would immediately pass my contact details to her producer who would, in turn, contact me very shortly.

That he did; Meirion Jones phoned me and, unknowingly, burst my bubble of hope when he explained that he worked on the *Newsnight* programme and planned to do a piece exposing Jimmy Savile as a paedophile. Swallowing my groan of dismay at my crushed plans and the tears that came with them, I explained to him that I had cancer, was extremely unwell and certainly did not feel strong enough or competent to undertake such an interview. Of course, Meirion was disappointed; he told me he'd been following my life story on FanStory.com and that, furthermore, Miss Jones, the headmistress of Duncroft, was his aunt. He began to win me over when he praised my writing and told me that, through my words, he felt as if he'd travelled back in time so that he could see, hear and smell everything I had described so accurately. Although I've never been good at accepting praise, his words flattered me (as they were, no doubt, intended to) and rather than hanging up the phone as I should have done I continued the conversation with Meirion, although at that point, I still insisted I could not do any interviews.

Meirion asked me why I had waited until recently to expose Savile. I replied that, in my opinion, I hadn't exposed him at all and neither had I intended to; I'd never made any secret of what had occurred between myself and the disgusting old pervert. Throughout my lifetime I'd told numerous people about it and found no one had been remotely surprised. That I'd ended up writing it all down had been due to encouragement from my psychologist in order for me to deal with a horrendous childhood and, anyhow, I had kept his identity more or less protected by using only his initials. I added that in any case my 'audience' was almost entirely American and that nobody over there knew of Jimmy Savile.

I should have heard alarm bells when Meirion gently pointed out that he wasn't an American and, furthermore, he had been directed to FanStory.com by another British reader. It was quite possibly only because I really didn't expect to be alive to have to deal with any backlash that I failed to hear the clear warning he'd given me: anybody could read my work; anybody could download my work; anybody could take my work and do with it whatever they wanted. However, I am pathetically naive in technological matters (as well as many ordinary life matters) and I missed the clues Meirion gave me as to the possible dangers or consequences of leaving what I'd written online and unprotected. I was entirely focused on having cancer and rather than really think about what Meirion wanted to do, my mind had already gone off to worry itself stupid once more over the prospect of my dropping dead and not leaving anything nice for my boys.

Although I held out against the proposed interview during that first telephone conversation, I was to become less and less resolute over the next few days. I spoke to my sons and to Peter and told them how absolutely gutted I felt that, after all, my book was not going to be turned into a BBC production and that Meirion was only interested in exposing the recently deceased Savile as a paedophile and pervert. My sons agreed that Savile had been that and moreover that they had noticed all manner of headlines extravagantly praising him, almost as if he were a saint. I told my family that, in my opinion, Savile would never be exposed for what he truly had been because it wouldn't be permitted to happen. I knew the old perv had had friends in high places, up to and including a British prime minister and royalty; therefore, in order to protect such important people, the truth would simply have to remain buried. In fact, several times I told Meirion Jones that he was labouring under a false impression that he could expose Savile, particularly since he worked for the BBC, an institution that openly almost worshipped the eccentric and revolting old creep.

After around five telephone calls between Meirion and myself, I finally agreed to do an interview, on camera, with Liz MacKean, a very well-respected journalist then also working for *Newsnight*. Almost as soon as I agreed to talk, things began to move incredibly quickly. Obviously, it was vital to Meirion that he get my interview on video before I changed my mind but also, as he pointed out, because the BBC had planned to do a host of TV shows over the festive season in which Savile would be praised and lauded, something he sincerely wished to put a stop to.

There was a mad flurry of activity at my home prior to the *Newsnight* team arriving. Cleaning had become something I was almost entirely unable to deal with and the place was full of heaps of clothing belonging to all of us which had been washed but never put away; all manner of clutter and junk had also accumulated, over time, and it all needed to be cleared away. Dust lay about a quarter of an inch thick on every flat surface and this also had to be dealt with. My sons and Peter worked like slaves to make the place presentable; in fact, my only worry in the run-up to the interview itself was that people might judge me on the poor state of my home! Cleaning was relatively straightforward, but getting rid of the scent of cats proved impossible. Peter insisted there was no scent, as did the boys, but I could smell it. I knew it was caused by cats spraying, marking their territory, year upon year in the same places and as such, it had soaked well into wood and plaster, and that short of ripping out all the floors, windows, skirting-boards and plaster there was virtually no way of dealing with the lingering aroma of 'eau de cat widdle'. We did our very best with air fresheners and just had to hope that our esteemed guests would not choke to death on the dubious mixture.

I cannot honestly say I felt nervous of the impending interview. After all, I had much more serious matters to worry about and simply speaking to someone could hardly be particularly stressful; it was more of an annoying interruption to my self-absorption. In any event, I felt absolutely secure in the knowledge that, even if I did the interview, something or someone would prevent it ever going on air. Whilst waiting for Meirion and Liz to arrive I reflected, somewhat sadly, that I was probably only doing the interview in order to make Meirion give up and leave me alone so that I could concentrate on the truly serious business of getting dead, even if I had nothing to leave behind for my sons!

Chapter Fourteen

Location: Court 13, Royal Courts of Justice, Strand, London

Timeline: 18 June 2015 – day four of the case

brave: *adjective*: 'Possessing or exhibiting courage or courageous endurance.'

At least I was able to sit safely between Peter and Helen that morning and could not be quite so openly scrutinised by all and sundry, although the couple of reporters close by had an extremely good view of me. I actually felt uncomfortably warm in spite of the air-conditioning in the room and, had it not been so vital for me to conceal my multiple tattoos, I'd have discarded both my jacket and the scarf Helen had lent me.

My thoughts drifted and, even though when I had worked, it had nearly always been within a legal environment, I found myself pondering upon the concept that everything about appearing in court felt elegiac. When had society decided, I wondered, that to appear as solemn and respectful, one must needs suffer funereal attire so depleted in colour that one may well have travelled back in time a hundred or more years? At least I didn't have to wear a wig and a long gown or a stiff collar and cravat like the QCs had to.

Once the judge arrived and everybody had returned to their seats, it was time for Meirion Jones to be cross-questioned. I felt quite surprised as he walked toward the witness box for he didn't look the same as I remembered him; he'd lost some weight and his hair had greyed significantly. But in spite of that, his eyes remained lively and intelligent and, as soon as he spoke, to confirm his name and details, I recalled his voice.

My legal team had told me that Meirion no longer worked for the BBC; he'd been dismissed, as had everybody who'd taken any part in the attempted and failed exposure of Jimmy Savile. Most people had simply found themselves jobless, but a lucky few had been moved to other departments within the corporation, and a couple, I was told, had taken early retirement. I made no remarks to my team about my thoughts on those job losses and changes, but I'd said in private, to Peter, that it seemed very, very odd to me (although at the same time, sad) that the BBC, being such an enormous entity, apparently intent on uncovering the whole and absolute truth of all and any abuses suffered at the hands of anyone connected to it, and keen for the general public to hold it once again in the highest regard, had treated its former employees so shamefully.

Peter retorted that they'd pretty much treated me as shamefully, or more so, by having left me isolated and having to find someone to defend me when, according to their own principles and guidelines, they should have looked after me as a vulnerable contributor. Peter was right, of course he was.

My whole team echoed those thoughts and feelings and had been astounded to discover that no form of indemnity existed between myself and the BBC in spite of their wordy 'code of practice'. Seeing how the BBC employees had been treated only added to the feelings of outrage and disappointment I felt. Actually, it looked to me as if Meirion was probably far happier in whatever job he had now. I found it interesting that, like me, he refused to take an oath on the Bible, and instead simply affirmed that he would speak the truth.

Mr Dunham peered down his nose at the former *Newsnight* producer as if he were something vaguely unpleasant which had, nonetheless, to be dealt with. In fact, Mr Dunham asked several pretty feeble questions at first, perhaps doing so in order to make Meirion feel that he could outdo the legal man and so make some kind of error later in the proceedings. I might well be being extremely uncharitable in making that observation.

Certainly, in Meirion Jones's tone of voice I thought I could detect more than a small amount of anger. Whether this was due solely to the fact that I'd been brought to court at all or for that and other reasons, I had no idea. In our brief interaction, both on the telephone and in person, I had found Meirion to be an honest, principled man. He'd told me, for example, how he and his parents had been deeply suspicious at the time of Savile's frequent visits to Duncroft. When they had expressed their concerns verbally to Miss Margaret Jones, Meirion's aunt and the headmistress of Duncroft at that time, a bitter family row had ensued that resulted in a rift which was to last many, many years.

During questioning, Meirion revealed how his attention had been brought by an investigative journalistic colleague to my memoirs on FanStory.com. He told the court how he'd read my descriptions of the building and grounds, members of staff, including his aunt, and found them to be exceptionally accurate. The very brief portion that referred to the celebrity visitor 'JS' only confirmed everything he and his parents had ever suspected. He instantly knew who JS must be, not just from the initials, he said, but also from the descriptions of his vehicle, appearance and mannerisms.

To my surprise, I discovered whilst Meirion answered the questions put to him, that he and his colleagues had initially thought me mistaken about the shows I attended as a guest of Jimmy Savile. They had felt entirely certain that I meant I'd been invited onto the show *Jim'll Fix It* because they hadn't been able to recall the show *Clunk Click*. Quite a reasonable proportion of time and research had ensued, meaning researchers had to dig through the archived old files at the BBC to unearth those shows to which I referred in my memoir.

Apparently, even before any evidence had been found to corroborate my story, Meirion and his team had worked out who the 'G' to whom I referred must be: Gary Glitter. In fact, since the man was already a convicted paedophile there was no new news to be had from that. Meirion told Mr Dunham that none of them working on the planned exposé of Savile had had any clue as to who the 'F' I referred to might be. Apparently, the clue 'popular comedian' had not made them consider the Claimant. Meirion reeled off a list of male celebrities' names which began with the letter F and said that he felt certain Mr Dunham could see the difficulty. Besides, Meirion pointed out, the Claimant was, in his opinion, less of a comedian and more a minor celebrity who was far more noted for his television appearances on the 'other' channel, another reason why they were unable to guess to whom I referred. Mr Dunham queried the phrase 'not a comedian' in an almost sarcastic tone and Meirion simply shrugged and replied that the Claimant had never made him laugh. Peter, seated beside me, wasn't the only person who suppressed a touch of laughter at that statement.

I, along with just about everybody else in the courtroom, could tell that Mr Dunham was more than a little irritated to hear Meirion state that from my memoir alone, nobody could guess who 'F' might have been. A large part of the case against me was that I'd deliberately defamed and libelled the Claimant within the pages of my memoir, which was freely available online. What Meirion Jones told the court would seem to show that the device I had employed to mask the identity of the man who had so badly humiliated me worked extremely well: on reading my memoir alone, nobody would have been able to identify the Claimant as the man to whom I referred. Thus, it appeared (to me) that, at the very least, there were surely no further grounds on which to continue with that part of the case against me. I'm not sure Mr Dunham agreed. Eventually, he asked the question of Meirion direct: How had he discovered the identity of 'F'? Of course, Meirion replied that he'd asked me and I'd told him, but only after extracting a binding promise from him not to reveal that information on camera in his exposé. Since the work he was doing at the time for *Newsnight* revolved solely around Savile, Meirion saw no reason not to give his word. In fact, Meirion told the court, he had been stunned to learn of the identity of 'F' not least because he was not an entertainer who would normally be associated with the BBC since he more often appeared on the independent channels. He added that it would have been virtually impossible for anybody to have worked out who I had written about, other than Savile.

Mr Dunham pointed out that his client had been shown on television, in relation to me, in a programme made by *Panorama*, also for the BBC, and aired in 2012. This programme had apparently been made in order to investigate what had occurred at the time of my interview with Meirion and to endeavour to find out why the planned *Newsnight* exposé had not gone ahead. Only when Meirion replied to that question did I realise just how badly he himself had been treated by the powers that be at the British Broadcasting Corporation. Not only had he been refused any input at all in the making of the *Panorama* documentary, he had been actively excluded from it. Therefore, his verbal promise to me, that in no way would he or his colleagues identify the Claimant, held no sway and had, in fact, been broken by the *Panorama* team.

Mr Dunham did not look well satisfied with that reply and he continued to question Meirion Jones on every tiny aspect of his interaction with me. Meirion stated that, in his opinion, I had done a great public service by being a part of the exposure of Savile. He referred to the 'bravery' it took to speak out on camera when nobody else would and sticking to my guns despite intense pressures from a media gone mad. Of course, I didn't agree with Meirion's viewpoint. I certainly have never considered myself to be brave – stupid, most definitely; naive, absolutely. But brave? Certainly not. Actually, I'd describe myself as probably one of the world's greatest cowards for I am afraid of virtually everything and everybody.

The questions continued and Meirion Jones continued to answer them concisely and without hesitation. Once again my thoughts drifted and I found myself pondering mortality. In the end, had not I given the interview quite simply because I'd felt entirely positive that I'd not be around to have to have to observe or take part in the inevitable media storm that would follow the exposure of the National Treasure that was Jimmy Savile? I scowled to myself. I'd not only remained alive but had ended up sitting in a courtroom some two hundred miles from my home watching whilst practically everybody who had come into contact with me was publicly torn to shreds.

I heard, as a kind of background commentary to my thoughts, Meirion Jones affirm that I had never sought publicity of my own accord and at no time, to his knowledge, had I ever received any kind of remuneration for the statements I'd made. Once again my thoughts veered in a new direction: it appeared that almost everyone in my local area had automatically assumed that I'd been paid for my story to both *Newsnight* and *Panorama*. In general, I had been viewed as a 'gold-digger' in regard to the whole Savile/abuse business; it would only be a very small step for people to further assume that I was attempting to extract money from the Claimant, when in fact, nothing could be further from the truth. I managed to more or less suppress a deep sigh as I concluded that people can only judge one another by their own standards. It had not occurred to me to ask for any kind of payment for the 'story'. As far as I was concerned, any money I might make out of the whole business would be whatever I could earn through my own writing efforts – in short, not a great deal!

When, at last, Meirion's ordeal ended and he left the witness stand I found myself pathetically grateful for having had his support and I wished, sincerely, that I could thank him, but I knew it could not happen, at least not that day and not within the confines of the court. Shortly after he'd left, the judge called a recess for lunch and, by the time Peter and I had finished discussing Meirion's evidence with David, who felt very pleased with how the ex-producer had come across, Meirion was long gone from the building.

Peter again led me across the busy Strand to Pret A Manger, which had become our regular lunch venue and, once in possession of sustenance, we found a quiet table tucked away in the far corner where we were able to quietly discuss the morning in court. After lunch, Mr Dunham would be cross-questioning Mark Williams-Thomas, to whom I had given an interview on camera. I had nothing like as much confidence in Mark Williams-Thomas as I'd had in Meirion Jones; I had no idea at all as to how he might come across. That coming afternoon felt, to me, the most stressful part of the trial so far.

Chapter Fifteen

Location: inside my own psyche

Timeline: *circa* 1973–2012

resilience: *noun*: 'Ability to recover readily from illness, depression, adversity, or the like; buoyancy.'

I think people believe they are paying me a compliment when they tell me how amazed they are at my resilience. I've never taken the remark as such; in fact, it tends to make me grind my teeth somewhat because, evidently, there is little to no understanding of me as a real person. I would never have described myself in such a way because I actually spend a good portion of my time expecting current situations to damage or kill me, a great deal of time and effort worrying about possible future situations which might frighten me to death, damage me irreversibly or kill me, all interspersed with uncontrollable and unpredictable flashbacks into my past, which erupt between the anxieties like pimples on scar tissue – and the rest of the time wishing I could stop the world and simply step off.

In point of fact, the only reason I am still walking upon this earth at all is very simple: I don't know how not to survive.

Surviving became a filthy habit of mine from a very, very early period in my life and I just don't know how to stop doing it, much as I often want to. Nobody would have been more delighted to wake one morning and find me dead (if also utterly pissed off by my thoughtlessness – where would she find the time to fill in all the forms and deal with all the aftermath?) than Mother. She'd told me often enough by the time I was three how my being born had utterly ruined her life and, sadly, that litany didn't stop when she married my stepfather. It actually got far worse because, once Mother had her longed-for baby boy, all she really wanted was for me to simply drop down dead or vanish. The feeling was more or less mutual; even though I desperately yearned for Mother's love and approval, she taught me to hate and fear her instead. I was to become Mother's whipping boy and carry upon my little shoulders everything she hated, regretted and got wrong, or simply blamed for the way she felt. There is a more than small chance that, had Nana not been a part of my life until I was around seventeen, survival would not have been possible for me. I truly believe that if Nana not been such a presence in the background, one of the beatings would have resulted in my death and Mother (possibly her husband too) would have ended up in jail.

I've thought, long and hard, about suicide throughout my lifetime. Not simply 'Oh, I wish I were dead', but seriously, in great detail. That sounds terribly melodramatic and self-centred, and perhaps it is. The trouble with suicide, though, is that it isn't actually an easy way out at all. For a start, if one is not absolutely successful, the aftermath is abominable. How truly dreadful to feel so totally useless, helpless, worthless and unwanted, only to fail in the attempt at taking one's own life? No wonder people who try to kill themselves end up within the mental-health system being observed by psychiatrists, psychologists and a whole gamut of well-meaning but usually entirely clueless people. The other matter to consider if one intends to 'end it all' is that the body, entirely independently of the mind, will strive always for life. Therefore, methods of self-disposal that are not doomed to failure are pretty limited. If one also factors in the desire to do the dreadful deed without involving anybody else who might be traumatised (drivers of vehicles, dog walkers, family members, for instance), then suicide becomes even more of a problem. For sure, I have considered every possible method, location and possible aftermath. Nobody wants to find a dead body, particularly not one which has lain undiscovered for a long period of time. Although I often dreamed of dying, slipping easily out of life, escaping forever from the misery, violence and paralysing fear that made up the sum total of my existence, what might happen after the event usually made me stall and further think things through. If I could have been absolutely certain that it would only ever be Mother who found my mortal remains, I'd have not hesitated to do away with myself in the most disgusting and messy way I could think of. I am more than aware of the probable psychology behind that thought and therefore, for no other reason than I consider myself to be above petty revenge, it has caused me to ponder further, on more than one occasion, to ensure I face the actual reality of death and not the puerile notion of 'they'll all be sorry when I'm dead'.

When I think back to those terrible days of my young childhood, often spent either locked in my tiny room in first, the caravan, and then in the horrid little hovel in Ludham, it is still far too easy for me to close my eyes and *feel* just as terrified, impotent and trapped as I did then. I cannot, of course, recall the exact thoughts I had, but even attempting to describe those feelings accurately is difficult if not impossible. Probably only those who might truly understand and grasp the horror are other survivors. So, overwhelming terror becomes, itself, like a crutch. If someone were to magically remove it, could I have continued to survive without it? Probably not is the answer to that particular possibility. Maybe fear was one of the mysterious factors that kept me alive.

Loneliness is often thought to be one of the main reasons why people try to kill themselves. Loneliness and isolation are powerful negatives to be sure, but in my particular case, I wasn't even fully aware of how lonely I had always been, or even how utterly isolated I was in regard to the world at large, until I began to heal. Of course that sounds preposterous: everyone knows when they're lonely, surely? To that query I can throw back the old cliché: 'You never know what you've missed if you've never had it to begin with.' Certainly, throughout my early childhood, I had no reason to believe that life was any different for me than it was for everybody else. Once I started school, however, my differences became apparent to me and that is when I began to learn how much damage Mother had already done – although it didn't begin to prepare me for what was still to come.

Chapter Sixteen

Location: Court 13, Royal Courts of Justice, Strand, London

Timeline: 18 June 2015 – day four of the case

goose: *noun*: *(slang)*: 'A poke between the buttocks to startle.'
goose: *verb*: *(slang)* 'To poke (a person) between
the buttocks to startle.'

Mark Williams-Thomas took the witness stand after lunch. He swore his oath on the Bible and sat down looking as well-groomed and confident as ever. I'd been told that he was a former police officer and had been involved in any number of abuse cases. Whatever had made him leave the police force and turn journalist I couldn't fathom. I disliked the man intensely, not least because of what he'd put me through, and I still couldn't understand why, when I eventually decided to speak out, I had selected him as the person to whom I would talk.

I would never even have been aware of Mark Williams-Thomas's existence had he not begun to contact me in the early new year of 2012. Unfortunately for me, although I had survived the cancer operation, I'd had some pretty horrendous complications and had been sent home with a gaping wound 20cm by 15cm, by 5cm deep, in my abdomen, which was in itself terrifying. One does not expect to be able to look down and see into one's innards, no matter how ill. And I was ill, desperately ill. My bed had been brought downstairs into the living room and I was confined to it, not by any instruction but purely by the fact of being too weakened, frail and ill to get out of it. District nurses came every day to change the packing and the dressing on my wound, and sometimes they needed to call more than once because there were additional problems with the stoma – not only had the stitches holding the stoma in place dehisced, leaving an additional wound beneath the stoma itself, but there was insufficient intact skin between the stoma and the gaping great wound for the stoma pouch to adhere to. This meant that with the smallest of movements from me the pouch detached itself in whole or in part and liquid faeces flowed into the open wound. I had a vast cocktail of drugs to take every day, including strong painkillers, antibiotics, anti-emetics and many others. In addition to that, every day a district nurse injected into my abdomen (away from the wound) an anti-clotting agent because I was bed-bound. I weighed under eight stone, looked as skeletal as a holocaust victim, had no appetite, felt absolutely grim and the big, black dog of depression had me engulfed utterly in a bleakness of spirit from which there seemed no escape.

Mark Williams-Thomas had made his first call to my landline in early January of 2012, whilst the district nurse was present dressing my wound. Peter had taken the call. He'd been angry and surprised and had told Mr Williams-Thomas that I was extremely unwell and unable to speak with him. A couple of days later, ever persistent, as reporters often are, he had called my mobile phone and I had answered. Although weak and weary beyond words, I'd been adamant that I could not talk to him about the Savile affair and had passed the phone to Peter, who in turn had told Mr Williams-Thomas again to leave me alone.

Later that same day, my landline telephone rang frequently and, time and again, no matter who answered the thing, a reporter would ask to speak to me and begin asking questions even before they were told I was too unwell to converse; several barely introduced themselves. All were dismissed, at first simply firmly and after a few hours, rudely. The following day, my mobile phone began to ring incessantly too. Often the display read 'Withheld' or 'Unavailable', but mostly it revealed unfamiliar mobile phone numbers. I'd answered the first couple of calls but very quickly became upset, especially since none of the callers was prepared to divulge from where they had obtained my number. That January was when I had to switch off both my landline and my mobile just to endeavour to maintain a modicum of peace. Mark Williams-Thomas had then contacted me by email, as had several other journalists. The upshot of this was that I could then add trapped, beleaguered and hopeless to my descriptors of how I was doing; being hounded by the media is not at all conducive to recovery. In any event, I held the deepest suspicion that Mark Williams-Thomas was somehow responsible for the media getting hold of my contact details, although, until my legal team began digging in preparation for the court case, I didn't know how this had occurred. I felt no better when I did know.

Mr Dunham asked Mr Williams-Thomas how he had become aware of me and what I'd had to say about Sir Jimmy Savile. Mr Williams-Thomas explained how Meirion Jones had contacted him during the latter part of 2011 as he'd been aware of his previous work with abuse victims and the fact that he was an ex-police officer. Meirion Jones had considered Mr Williams-Thomas to be an appropriate person to engage as a consultant for the programme he planned to make. Apparently, there were a great many discussions and, although there were plenty of other alleged victims of Savile, none wished to speak out on the record, at it were. It was felt that if they could only get me to speak, on camera, they might have enough evidence, along with the testimony of those others who were not prepared to reveal themselves, to make a programme exposing Savile as a serial paedophile.

Mr Dunham paused and studied the papers on the lectern in front of him. There followed a good many questions from him relating to Savile and how the team – Meirion Jones, Liz MacKean and Mark Williams-Thomas – had intended to reveal the true nature of the eccentric fundraiser. It turned out that I was the only person they had who was prepared to waive my right to anonymity and go on camera with my allegations (something I had not known at the time because I'd been told that there were 'other victims', all of whom, in my naivety, I'd assumed would also be doing television interviews). Very many questions followed about how other victims had been contacted, why I'd been approached by *Newsnight* (mainly because of my memoir online) and then there was a mention of the 'other perpetrators'. I'm certain Mr Williams-Thomas ground his teeth at some of Mr Dunham's questions because many of them seemed, even to a layperson like me, to be rather simplistic or unnecessary.

When, at last, Mr Dunham asked Mr Williams-Thomas if he had known the identity of the person I'd referred to as 'F' in my memoir, Mr Williams-Thomas shook his head and replied that he had not; not until after I'd given my interview had he become aware of my naming of the Claimant and then only after he had spoken with Ms MacKean and Meirion Jones. He further explained that, having seen the interview and read the relevant section of my memoir, he'd had no reason to believe I was telling anything other than the plain truth. He also pointed out to Mr Dunham that I had never, at any stage, sought any kind of compensation or even an apology from the Claimant.

The cross-examination then turned to the matter of how the programme had been 'pulled' at the last minute. Apparently, Peter Rippon, responsible for having given Meirion and Liz the original go-ahead to make the programme, suddenly objected and said that from what he'd seen of the interview with me, there was absolutely no evidence to corroborate what I'd said. Of course, Meirion Jones was furious; he had already shared with Peter Rippon the suspicions he and his family had held in the early seventies when they'd seen Savile visiting Duncroft. Despite the best efforts of everybody involved, Mr Rippon found further objections and the more the team pressed to be permitted to continue, the more firmly they were refused. Mark Williams-Thomas went on to explain how he had become 'redundant' in that without a programme, they did not need a consultant, and so he had taken the findings and approached the independent television channel to see if they would be prepared to continue with it.

As this was explained, I couldn't help but scowl and clench my jaw in frustrated fury. I felt absolutely certain that it was, at the very least, unethical for Mark Williams-Thomas to have taken all my details (and probably everybody else's too), but more, I felt in some bizarre way violated. Had not the BBC had a duty of care to me? I'd been so very vulnerable at the time I'd been approached; sick with cancer, not expecting to survive, anxious, depressed, hopeless, not to mention all the other problems I'd had to try to live with. I so wanted Mr Dunham to make some kind of statement that the BBC had been wrong to permit Mr Williams-Thomas to take the information and contact details, but of course, that was not what we were in court for and the cross-examination continued. Like it or not, I had to just accept that my personal contact details and other private matters had been so valueless to those at the BBC that they tossed them away without a second thought. Mr Williams-Thomas did manage to point out that he'd been aware of the fact that I'd told Meirion Jones and Liz MacKean that they simply would not be permitted to expose Savile and how my prediction had proved to be spot-on. Mr Dunham asked him why he thought that might be and, of course, Mark

Williams-Thomas had to reply that anything he said would be pure speculation rather than hard fact and, therefore, it would not be reasonable for him to make any kind of statement on why the programme might have been ditched.

It seemed to take forever for Mr Dunham to get around to when Mark Williams-Thomas had begun to contact me. Actually, when spoken of in the court, it didn't sound at all like the invasion it had been. Mr Williams-Thomas said that he spoke to me on several occasions by telephone but that I was 'not willing' to discuss matters with him and that I frequently became extremely angry and upset so, in the end, he had gone ahead and made his *Exposure* documentary without any input from me. Mr Dunham practically pounced on that statement and asked for further clarification: had Ms Ward not appeared in the documentary? Of course, I had not done so, and Mr Williams-Thomas confirmed this, something that seemed to perplex Mr Dunham somewhat. During the run-up to the actual court hearing David and Helen had both repeated, several times, to Mr Dunham that I had not taken part in the making of the *Exposure* documentary, but this fact never truly seemed to have settled in the Claimant's team's collective awareness. Of course, I had *believed* I was being interviewed for the ITV *Exposure* documentary, but that juicy little gem of information had not yet surfaced.

Mr Williams-Thomas was asked why, in any case, had he felt it so important to speak with me about Savile and he explained that it had been due to having read my memoir online. I had been the only person to openly admit that any kind of wrongdoing went on at Duncroft, even though I'd only used the perpetrator's initials 'JS'. He had trawled through the Friends Reunited website and found a Duncroft sector, wherein he'd discovered several photographs of girls with Jimmy Savile and, more to the point, comments hinting that Savile was, at the very least, a 'dirty old man'. He had tried on many occasions to contact as many ex-Duncroft women as possible, he explained, but found that most had no wish to drag up old memories or speak to an investigative journalist. Also, he added, having seen the whole of the interview Ms MacKean had conducted with me, in which I'd come across so strongly, he'd wanted to endeavour to replicate it if he could; of course, I'd been extremely uncooperative.

Mr Dunham pointed out that Mr Williams-Thomas had, even so, managed to obtain an interview with me, on camera, during which I had made slanderous and untrue remarks about his client, amongst other revelations. Mr Williams-Thomas agreed that he had interviewed me and further explained that he'd been contacted by me 'out of the blue' just two days prior to his documentary going to air. He told Mr Dunham that he quickly made arrangements to visit me and get the interview before I changed my mind.

Being unable to enlighten Mr Dunham as to why I had suddenly changed my mind about speaking to him, Mr Williams-Thomas went on to detail how he had managed to get hold of a cameraman and a producer at short notice in order to attend at my home for the interview. Whilst he spoke of these matters I surreptitiously studied the judge who, unlike me, was paying careful attention to both questions and answers and making notes. I allowed myself to ponder how much hard work and concentration a judge had to input at any hearing and shuddered involuntarily. Helen leaned over to ask in a whisper whether I felt all right. I assured her of my good health and turned my attention back to the matter in hand.

Mr Williams-Thomas looked as if he might have eaten something unpleasant but was trying to hide his reaction from his hosts. I tried not to giggle, hurriedly disguising my snort of laughter as a sneeze. Mr Dunham was focusing on the part of the interview where I had said that his client had 'goosed' me. Having already closely questioned me on this matter, Mr Dunham knew that I'd been required to repeat the allegation no less than three times before Mr Williams-Thomas had been satisfied with the manner in which I'd phrased my accusation. Now he wanted to see if Mr Williams-Thomas would corroborate and further explain why this had been the case. Whilst there could be no denying that I'd been asked to repeat certain parts of the interview, trying to explain to Mr Dunham that Mr Williams-Thomas thought the general public might not comprehend the term 'goosed' turned out to be akin to trying to shout information to a stand of trees. It appeared that Mr Dunham simply could not understand, nor accept, Mr Williams-Thomas's assumption that most members of the public simply wouldn't have understood my meaning. This was extremely peculiar, in my opinion, because had I not had to explain to Mr Dunham myself, in minute detail, what 'goosed' and 'to goose' actually meant?

Mr Dunham frowned, stared at the papers in front of him once more and then drew a breath. 'So, what you're saying then, is that the interview with Ms Ward was staged?' he asked. Somebody gasped but I've no idea who it could have been. Mr Williams-Thomas fixed his questioner with a steely glare and replied, in a tone like glacial ice, that anyone who might accuse him of staging an interview would likely find himself facing a court battle of his own. Apparently unabashed and certainly in no way apologetic, Mr Dunham barely hid the satisfied smirk on his face. Had he truly endeavoured to offend and upset this witness? I wondered.

When the questions turned to the matter of the media reports that the Claimant had been at a party, hosted by Jimmy Savile and with Gary Glitter also present, Mr Williams-Thomas was quick to point out that to the best of his knowledge, I had never, ever claimed such a thing and he had not reported on it. He added, without prompting, that at no time had Gary Glitter and the Claimant been present together at BBC premises – at least, not as far as he knew and certainly not in relation to the Savile scandal that had unfolded.

Mr Dunham asked whether Mr Williams-Thomas had told me that he himself was building a dossier on his client. I felt sorely aggrieved when the hitherto perfect witness denied having said anything of the kind, adding that to say such a thing would be unprofessional in the extreme. I glanced at Peter and could see, from the expression he wore, that he too recalled what Mr Williams-Thomas had said: Peter had been present at the interview. To my astonishment, Mr Williams-Thomas then went on to deny that he was working on anything at all to do with the Claimant. This was the first time anything I'd said had not been totally corroborated by Mr Williams-Thomas; everything else had been confirmed completely. I tried, very hard, not to allow despondency a foothold, but it crept into my psyche nonetheless; the big, black dog that is depression never has far to run to find me.

I realised the questions had changed and that Mr Dunham was now asking Mr Williams-Thomas about my age at the time of the alleged incident. The witness replied that I had been fifteen years old when the event occurred. Mr Dunham quickly pointed out that not only had several newspapers reported I'd claimed to have been fourteen, but that I'd also said so in one interview, on camera; apparently, this would seem to imply that I was less than truthful. To my intense relief, Mr Williams-Thomas replied to the effect that, as far as he'd been aware, and from reading my memoir, I'd said I was fourteen when I first went to Duncroft and that the incident had taken place shortly before I left (after I'd turned sixteen). Once again, as the two argued over minutiae, my awareness of the court faded and I drifted into my darkest memories, which made me shiver involuntarily. Peter reached down and squeezed my fingers briefly, returning my attention to the matters in hand.

I studied Mark Williams-Thomas as he sat in the witness box. His body language gave nothing away and I thought perhaps he'd studied enough about that particular 'science' to be able to position himself exactly as he desired. He had kept a level tone throughout – save for that one testy reply in relation to 'staged' interviews – and yet he had made no attempt to hide his anger. I pondered that silently for a while and missed a few of the last questions asked of him.

Evidently Mr Williams-Thomas had been in court enough times before to make him aware of how things one said might be twisted, by a skilful questioner, in order to make it appear that something entirely different had been meant. On every single occasion, when Mr Dunham asked a question and then questioned or misinterpreted the answer, Mr Williams-Thomas was just as quick to respond in kind. Grudging admiration caused me to shake my head slightly, although I didn't smile.

Finally, and quite abruptly, the interview ended and Mr Williams-Thomas was given permission to leave the witness stand. He didn't linger; neither did he even glance in my direction or acknowledge me in any way. I became aware once again of feeling uncomfortably hot and more than simply tired; I was exhausted and I knew, given the opportunity, I'd sleep right there in the courtroom.

Even recognising my extreme fatigue as stress-induced and exacerbated by the waves of depression that continued to wash over me, I felt panicked: what if I passed out? Nausea and a wave of dizziness, also stress-induced, caused me to grab at Peter's hand. He didn't pull away, even though my hands were clammy. We stood whilst the judge retired from the court and waited to listen to something David needed to tell us, although I have to confess, my ears were ringing and I had little clue as to what was said. I nodded and smiled and agreed to something or another and then followed Peter, Helen, David and Yinka from the courtroom and down the back stairs.

Outside, it was extremely hot but I couldn't remove either my scarf or jacket until Peter had hailed us a taxi and it had pulled out of sight of the few press reporters and photographers lingering outside the courts. A picture of me with all my skin-art revealed at this stage wouldn't, I thought, be helpful.

Chapter Seventeen

Location: at home in Shropshire

Timeline: *circa* 1999–2001

neurosis: *noun*: 'Also called psychoneurosis. A functional disorder in which feelings of anxiety, obsessional thoughts, compulsive acts, and physical complaints without objective evidence of disease, in various degrees and patterns, dominate the personality.'

Being mentally ill is not fun. Let me rephrase and clarify that statement: when one is mentally unwell, fun does not exist; nothing positive exists any more. Laughter, enthusiasm, hope, even general day-to-day plans, all vanish into a miasma of negativity; in my case, this mostly manifested itself as fear. It's difficult to explain in a way that an unaffected person can begin to understand how very normal, everyday things can become enormous obstacles and objects of terror. For example, not only was I frightened of eating and drinking (the emetophobia had become completely unmanageable at this point) but also of going to the lavatory, sleeping, interacting with other people – even my own children – absolutely everything one might do on an ordinary day became an obstacle of insurmountable dread.

Dr Robert Greaves and his wife, Dr Judy Greaves, were both concerned with my care and recovery. Several times, one or the other visited me at home to check that I was all right. Of course, in the beginning, I had no concept of how much time and attention was being lavished on me by my doctors. At that stage, I trusted them no more than I trusted anyone else... basically, not at all. My poor children must have been so hurt by my suspiciousness of every little kindness they offered me, although I'm sure that all the professionals involved had probably seen it all before and been unconcerned by it. I can tell you, it is no easy matter to admit that one's intellect has completely jumped ship and left behind only paranoia, suspicion and abject fear. I continued to try to reason with myself but I was unable to hold any thoughts together for longer than a fleeting few seconds; the fear was simply too overwhelming and powerful.

I found my first few appointments with the psychologist and community psychiatric nurses, quite simply, terrifying. Not only had I to leave the house to attend them, something else I'd become phobic about doing, but I felt so entirely vulnerable being in a strange place with people I didn't know – bearing in mind, even people I'd known all my life had become frightening to me. I'd totter out of the taxi, a CPN on either side to help keep me upright, and then, once inside, even after being presented with a cup of hot, strong tea and placed in a comfortable chair, I could only sit and shiver violently as the terror held me in a vice-like grip.

I'm not aware of when, precisely, I began to improve, only

that it took a very, very long time. Of course, one of the very first facts I became aware of as the self-absorbed panic began to lessen was of how my poor kids had not only looked after themselves and each other but me as well. That same awareness brought with it yet another great burden of guilt to add to those I'd been hauling around for most of my lifetime. Dr Carolyn McQueen, my designated psychologist, proved to be not only extremely clever but also patient, methodical and, above all, showed me such empathy that I began to trust her... a little.

Of course, the psychologist knew very well how gently making me turn and confront the issues would, eventually, begin to heal my battered and bruised psyche. She made no secret of her admiration for me in that I'd survived, thus far, everything life and people had burdened me with and, having established the details of some of my tried and tested 'coping mechanisms', she reminded me to begin to use them again. Progress was about as rapid as the movement of plate tectonics but it was, nevertheless, progress. Dr McQueen told me she had contacted a colleague of hers, a cognitive behavioural therapist who she felt might be able to help me with the emetophobia. I balked at the idea of having to attend somewhere new, and panicked when she informed me her colleague was male. The possible therapy was temporarily shelved.

In point of fact, I can't actually recall much of the period of my mental illness. Looking back, everything seems tangled and vague as if seen though a swirling fog. I'm sure I've forgotten an awful lot of important stuff. Time held very little meaning for me; I do recall that much. I kind of blundered through life, day to painful day, either punctuated by periods of not sleeping much at all or of resisting sleep for as long as possible and then tumbling straight into nightmares. I've often thought that if I'd written those dreams down I might have made a name as a writer of horror. I simply could not understand from where my brain generated such awful images and concepts. Frequently, in my dreams, I murdered everybody I cared about; in fact, my dream-self was a scarily strong, hard-faced and violent creature. Sometimes I saw myself as a dragon and at other times more like my actual self but with super-strength and a super-vindictive temper to match. Dr McQueen felt the dreams were probably my sub-conscious trying to reach through to aid me in the healing. Whilst she never interpreted my dreams herself, she did encourage me to think about them in a different way. Once again, this small nudge in the direction of good mental health had a positive effect.

During the same period, and whilst I gradually recovered from severe mental ill health, my body snuck up on me and began to behave in a totally unacceptable manner. Looking back, I think the physical symptoms began more or less at the same time as the mental-health stuff, and for that reason alone, I don't think I need take legal action against my doctors. They were perfectly entitled to believe my physical symptoms occurred as a direct result of the neuroses of my mental state. Of course, their assumption was wrong, as already mentioned, but it wasn't the fault of the doctors themselves. In fact, by the time Dr McQueen had deemed my mental state well enough healed that it could not be responsible for my physical symptoms, more than two years had passed. However, I had not healed so completely as to be brave enough to undergo the investigation the physicians wanted. As I've explained, I felt certain that any bowel preparation I was given would make me vomit and therefore I declined. As a matter of fact, not long after I'd refused the necessary investigation Dr McQueen's colleague visited me at home in order to see what CBT might be able to do for me.

Most phobias respond to cognitive behavioural therapy. Unfortunately for me, probably the most common phobia that does not is emetophobia. The problem in dealing with such a fear is that most CBT involves gradually increasing exposure to the feared object/situation. Since it is impossible to say, 'Right, then. Today, we'll just feel a little bit sick for five minutes. Tomorrow, we can increase that by a couple of minutes and the intensity of nausea experienced.' Well, of course, one can say that, but it would actually be impossible to achieve. The therapist himself was pleasant enough and, somehow, completely non-threatening. Over five sessions, all of them at my home, we discussed coping mechanisms, ways in which to face some of the things I feared and ways I might attempt to deal with them. He reassured me that the levels of panic and anxiety I felt would gradually lessen if I faced the terror head-on. Of course, I'd known that throughout my life, but I needed him to tell me if for no other reason than to remind me that I really could overcome most things life threw at me – for had I not already survived far, far more than the average person?

I continued to see Dr McQueen even when the acute phase

of my mental illness had largely resolved. Gradually, and without my even being aware of it, I became better and better. I interacted with my children once more, even though my relationship with the middle son had changed dramatically; we'd been very close prior to my breakdown, but as I recovered I realised he had withdrawn into himself and remained largely aloof. Actually, all relationships had changed; the middle son was the one I noticed first and easily the most dramatic change. Even though Dr McQueen had planted the seed in my mind that I should write about my life in order to heal, I felt far too busy at this stage to begin such a mammoth task. I had a home to run and a place to reclaim as the head of the household, never mind the emotional attachments that had become fragile enough to shatter if I didn't tend them with all diligence.

Coming back from such a catastrophic breakdown would prove to be one of the most intensive things I'd ever had to experience. There were regular setbacks, of course. Sometimes, I seemed to take two steps forward and then, inexplicably, half a dozen or more backwards. However, despite all that, little by little I did recover until I felt almost whole again, although of course, by that stage I'd realised that I had never, in fact, been 'whole' during my lifetime. Suddenly, I had so much ancient stuff to deal with that the urge to run forever often snatched at me. Again, I suffered with night terrors, vivid nightmares and waking flashbacks of moments from my past. Somehow, with the help of my doctors, various community psychiatric nurses, Dr McQueen, Rosemary (my best friend of thirty years plus), John (another, more recent friend) and, of course, Peter, who had just arrived in my life at that time, I very gradually recovered further. I still suffered periods of unexplained physical ill health, but even I believed all my symptoms were psychosomatic and so, even when I found myself confined not just to the house but to the smallest room in the house, I accepted it (however gracelessly). The doctors obligingly prescribed stronger anti-emetic drugs, which controlled both the nausea and the persistent heartburn fairly well, but nobody really spoke to me about it and I had no desire to stop taking the medication.

Life continued with the ordinary ups and downs one expects to experience, along with half a dozen or more disasters nobody could have predicted. I managed to survive them all and, in fact, coped extremely well in circumstances in which others assured me they'd have fallen apart. I had signed up to study for a bachelor's degree in earth sciences with the Open University at the beginning of my second year of seeing Dr McQueen. Of course, she had been the one to suggest I do so when I'd expressed regret one day at how I'd failed so miserably in science as a youngster, but had subsequently developed an avid interest in cosmology, physics, vulcanology, chemistry and geology, not to mention various other aspects of scientific discovery and progression. I had slipped so easily back into studying and learning that I'm quite certain it had a lot to do with the way I dealt with events. I did exceptionally well in the first year of study, which further boosted my confidence, particularly when the university sent me a certificate proving that I had completed level one of a degree course and earned a diploma in Natural Sciences as well as sixty points towards the three hundred and sixty points required for an honours degree.

It was, quite possibly, the beginning of studying for the degree that was the trigger for me to start writing about my life. I'd never owned a personal computer before and the Open University had a scheme which permitted one to purchase a refurbished machine with all the software necessary to study the course at a greatly reduced cost. More important for me was the fact that I could pay for the thing in small monthly instalments. Had it not been for this scheme I might never have obtained a computer and never begun to write.

Between assignments and studying, I tentatively began to write a bit. At first I wrote only fiction: short stories, a little poetry sometimes, plans for a longer piece of fiction sketched out in a Word document. I've always written stories and poetry, song lyrics and also one or two books. The first was when I was at boarding school, all handwritten and absolute rubbish; the others were handwritten and illustrated for my children. My physical infirmities didn't seem to matter much any more. I could still think, even if I was seated in the smallest room. When I finally emerged, whatever I'd thought about could be typed up on the computer.

I found much of my time would be spent seated at the computer, either on study and assignments or on the Open University site watching tutorials and video classes or writing. It felt good to have rekindled my creativity somewhat. Also, it was an extremely good way for me to distract myself from the thoughts I had about beginning all over again with a new psychologist, because Dr McQueen had left the mental health service for pastures new. I probably became rather distant once more from my children, but they didn't complain. At least I could spend time in the same room with them and hold a conversation, after a fashion.

I have no recall whatsoever about why I began to write my life story when I did. As I have said earlier, I just began to write one day whilst sitting at the computer. Since life has always been difficult and painful, I was not very far into the manuscript when I encountered my first memory of trauma. I wrote it; I felt it again; I raged; I grieved for the little girl I'd been without comfort or love; I raged some more. The youngest of my sons came in from school to find me tearful and furious, stamping about in the lounge, apparently shouting at an invisible person. Of course he was surprised; who wouldn't be? However, he took it in his stride and, when I explained, wisely told me that in reacting the way I had, I'd probably heal far more quickly.

And that was how it was. Every morning, I had something to get up for. I'd rush downstairs, breakfast, do the minimum of chores and then settle in front of the computer to write. Almost every day involved tears, rage, sorrow, panic, anxiety, frustration and a gamut of other emotions, some for which I have no name. The computer greedily ate the words I ploughed into it and the emotion poured out of me, into the air where it dissipated harmlessly like a noxious gas in a fresh breeze. I was, quite definitely, beginning to recover in a way far more thorough than simply learning how to function from day to day.

The new psychologist, Dr Isabel Goodwin, was very easy

to get along with and also to trust. She exuded calm and had a ready wit and sense of humour, which meant that, just occasionally, we could chuckle at something together. In any event, although her methodology was quite different to that of Dr McQueen, Dr Goodwin continued where her colleague had left off. Coupled with the writing, my healing from the effects of things which had occurred many, many years in the past gathered pace and even I could perceive the rapid changes within myself.

I had probably written around a quarter of a million words when I stumbled, quite by accident, on an internet site for writers, FanStory.com, which I first mentioned in an earlier chapter. It appeared to work as a kind of sounding board between authors and poets; one would upload one's work, other members would read it and then leave comments, mostly pointing out grammatical errors, punctuation, spelling and typos, although content was also included. The site had its own currency of 'member dollars', which could be earned by reading and reviewing others' work. Once enough member dollars had accrued, they could be used to upload and post one's own work for the other members to do likewise. I considered the membership fee of around five dollars (less than five pounds) to be well worth the advantage of not only obtaining feedback for my style and actual story, but also for assistance in things I may have been getting wrong grammatically. Therefore, I joined the site, spent two whole evenings reading poetry and other people's prose and, when I'd accrued enough member dollars, I posted up the first chapter of my biography, which I'd decided to call simply 'Keri' (the name I had been given as a child, even though it was not my real name, but had been added by baptism, something I did not find out until, aged eighteen, I applied for a birth certificate in order to get married). I went to bed that night wondering what comments, if any, I'd find the next morning, for most of the members appeared to be either American or Australian and the site itself was American. I found plenty of comments the next day, most of them complimentary of my style, all of them appalled at the treatment I'd suffered, and some few of them very usefully pointing out glitches in sentence structure and grammar.

From that day in January of 2009, my life took on a fairly rigid structure. By day I would intersperse writing with study, and in the evenings I read and commented upon other members' work, earning me the member dollars with which to post my next chapter. My healing took on a more frenetic pace; had it not been for Dr Goodwin, I may well have stumbled to a halt in the healing process, but she kept me going.

As I have said before, I've never had many friends; there have nearly always been 'trust issues'. In my personal case it is that I trust people far, far too easily, and often the very people who should not be trusted any further than one could spit a squirrel are the ones in whom I place my trust and faith. Thus, friendships rarely last long for me and most often end with me being hurt in some fundamental way. The exception which proves that rule is, of course, my best friend Rosemary. Quite suddenly, I found I had 'followers' or 'fans' on the FanStory

171

site and many of them extended a hand of friendship (albeit across an ocean and several continents in some cases). These new 'internet friends' encouraged me, consoled me, perked me up when I felt low or that I could not continue with the writing, and were some of the people in whom I confided when I needed to speak about matters that I couldn't discuss with my children. There were a great many private messages between myself and other members, some of whom I got to know very well indeed. Pseudonyms are used on the site and so, after a few weeks of speaking via personal messages, to be blessed with someone's real name was quite a compliment. Not everybody was so forthcoming, of course.

It was through these 'friends' that I learned of the 'NaNoWriMo challenge' – basically, a challenge to see if one could knock out a novel of fifty thousand words or more in just one month. Intrigued, I went to the site and after only a brief scan of the rules and how to take part, I signed up.

Generally, I wrote about five thousand words a day, sometimes on my life story, at other times, in short fiction for FanStory contests or even essays for my studies. I didn't think I'd have much problem in chucking in an extra couple of thousand words a day for the challenge and I didn't have a problem doing so. In fact, I thoroughly enjoyed myself and I continued to write my life story too. I 'won' a completely free proof of a paperback copy of my express-written and entirely unedited or corrected 'book'. The thing is, once I'd got my hands on that paperback book with my name on the front cover, even though I knew it to be absolute rubbish, I still experienced an intense pleasure and satisfaction in holding my own written work in my hands.

It was the holding of a piece of fiction that drew my attention to the fact that I could self-publish my biography through CreateSpace, should I desire to do so. After consulting with internet friends and Dr Goodwin, all of whom thought it was worth a try, particularly since it would cost me nothing (other than stress as I attempted to ply my feeble technological knowledge in order to format the manuscript as required by CreateSpace). Eventually, over a period of several weeks and with many, many false starts, it was finally done.

When the first 'proof' arrived it consisted of the maximum number of pages permitted, and with such minuscule print size the thing was barely legible. In short, I'd written way too much to produce a single volume. Rather than edit any of it away – after all, it was for me that I was producing the thing and it had been in order to heal me that I'd written it – I simply split it into two volumes. When those two proofs arrived, I was delighted and approved them immediately.

I knew the chances of my actually making any sales of the print-on-demand books were negligible. But at least I could put the volumes up on my bookshelf to serve, if not only for pure self-satisfaction, as a reason for continuing with the next volume, which was already under construction. I had no idea where I would stop writing; how could I choose? My whole life had involved me staggering from one painful disaster to another and on to yet more. Dr Goodwin simply shrugged and advised that I'd know when it was time to stop.

Chapter Eighteen

Location: Court 13, Royal Courts of Justice, Strand, London

Timeline: 19 June 2015 – day five of the case

credible: *adjective*: 1. 'Capable of being believed; believable: *a credible statement*.' 2. 'Worthy of belief or confidence; trustworthy: *a credible witness*.'

Peter and I arrived a little late to court on the morning of 19 June due to our taxi having become stuck in a traffic snarl-up that was the result of a collision. I did my level best to hurry up the stone staircase and along to Court 13, but I felt particularly short of breath on that day and so had to keep stopping to rest and breathe every half dozen or so steps.

When we finally arrived outside the court, I noticed a lady sitting alone on a bench against the wall. I did a double take before I recognised Liz MacKean. As soon as we recognised one another we smiled and she stood to approach me and give me a brief hug. I should have loved to have been able to spend some time with Liz but Peter interrupted our greetings and told us he thought we probably should not be speaking to one another at all. Chagrined, Liz and I parted without another word and I allowed Peter to lead me into the courtroom. Fortunately, the judge had not yet arrived so our tardiness had not interrupted proceedings.

I managed to whisper to Helen that I'd seen and greeted Liz outside the courtroom and she replied she was glad to hear that the witness had arrived, adding that Peter was quite correct in that I should not really have spoken to her. Feeling inexplicably guilty, I reached for the water and drank down a full glass before using my inhaler. I had no clue as to why I should be finding it harder to breathe on that particular day than on previous days. I didn't feel particularly nervous, just breathless.

At the close of the previous day's proceedings, there had been discussion between the judge and the two legal representatives because another Duncroft woman had been subpoenaed by my team to attend on the nineteenth, and she was neither happy to give evidence nor was she legally represented. I'd really not paid much attention to what was being said, as I'd been wallowing in guilt about it being entirely my fault she'd be put under the stress of coming to court; it wasn't as if the poor woman had even been a friend of mine back in 1974. As far as I could recall, although we muddled along reasonably well most of the time, we were not friends and I think she had held me in some contempt.

The judge had agreed that the witness could remain anonymous and given leave for a request to be made to the BBC to provide funding for counsel for her. The first matter of the day was, then, the judge's query as to whether or not

'Witness C' would be attending and whether or not the BBC had provided legal cover for her. David advised affirmative to both. At this stage, the judge turned his attention to the few journalists in court and told them that, under no circumstances, was the identity of the woman known as 'Witness C' to be made known publicly.

I kind of zoned out of the reality of the courtroom once again as I pondered how it could be that the BBC evidently felt perfectly happy to provide funding for counsel for Witness C but, even under extreme pressure from David and the rest of my team, had never been persuaded to assist me in defending myself in any way. Had it not been for David being prepared to take me on with a CFA (conditional fee arrangement) in place, I'd have been facing all of this with nobody beside me save Peter. I tried, somewhat unsuccessfully, to analyse my feelings on this matter. Did I feel jealous? I asked myself. Or perhaps angry or resentful? None of those feelings seemed to apply. Had anybody asked me, just then, how I felt about the way the BBC had treated me I'd have probably shrugged, more a defeatist gesture than anything else, and replied that I'd never really expected any better – from anyone.

When Liz MacKean took the witness stand I was aware enough to note, privately, that she made no religious vow to speak the truth. Whilst the first mundane questions were asked of her and she replied in her distinctive voice, I found myself thinking that she'd probably seen way too much nastiness to be able to believe in any omnipotent being remotely interested in what a group of daft mammals did to each other.

'So, you'd read Ms Ward's online account before you interviewed her?' The question from Mr Dunham hung in the air and brought my attention back to the courtroom. Ms MacKean agreed that had been the case; Meirion Jones had shown my work to her. Mr Dunham went on to ask whether or not she or Meirion, or indeed Mark Williams-Thomas, had been aware of the identity of either 'G' or 'F' prior to the interview going ahead. She patiently explained that none of the people working on the *Newsnight* exposé had worked out who 'F' might have been, but more than one had thought 'G' might have been Gary Glitter. In fact, Ms MacKean added, they had all been convinced I'd made a mistake because no one recalled the *Clunk Click* show; they thought I'd meant the other show Savile made, *Jim'll Fix It*. Even looking thorough archived recordings of that show, they were none the wiser as to the possible identity of 'F'.

Mr Dunham went on to ask several more questions about what Ms MacKean and her colleagues had read from the accounts I had written. I squirmed in my seat; I'd removed my memoir from the FanStory site as soon as the threat of legal action being taken against me had occurred. The more I listened to the things people said, the more I realised how incredibly foolish and naive I'd been in believing my writing to be secure, or even that anybody might be remotely interested enough to download it, share it or talk about it. It was all very well wanting to be a successful writer, I grumbled silently to myself, but I'd certainly never intended for my healing memoir to be what came to public attention.

Ms MacKean, meanwhile, was busy describing how she met me. She told the court that I was, quite obviously, extremely unwell and she added that she'd felt anxious about interviewing me when I was so poorly. She'd not seen anything signed by me by way of consent to broadcast or waiving my right to anonymity, she said, and then added that I'd been adamant she and Meirion would never be permitted to air the programme they were making, even though they both assured me their editor was aware of and right behind them.

Again, Mr Dunham asked why Ms MacKean thought I'd be so certain the programme would never go to air. She lifted an elegant shoulder and replied that I'd told her the 'bigwigs' and 'powers-that-be' at the BBC would simply not permit Savile to be exposed. At the time she'd thought I'd felt intimidated by the revelation being made public but, with hindsight, she now believed that I knew very well how the Corporation worked because my beliefs had proved accurate. I felt the blood rising up my neck and into my cheeks as she told the court this and sincerely hoped none of the journalists were watching me. I'd actually said all that, yes, but I'd added, at the time, 'at the risk of being labelled a "crazy conspiracy theorist". I wondered, as I tried to disperse the blush by controlled breathing, whether Meirion and Liz had actually wondered, at that stage, if I really was a bit of a nutcase.

Of all the witnesses I'd heard thus far, I was more interested in what Liz MacKean had to say than any of the others. Even so, I did think she made far too much of me and what I'd told her of my sojourns at the BBC theatre and the company of Jimmy

Savile. More than once, she described me and the things I'd told her as 'utterly credible' and 'entirely believable'. A brief stab of bitterness hit me when she said that: if *only* I'd been believed as a youngster, at any stage of my existence, then life would have been completely different for me. On the other hand, since I believe we each are the sum total of our basic genes and the entirety of our experience, I wouldn't be the person I am had I been believed.

The cross-examination continued and Mr Dunham asked Ms MacKean about the identity of 'F', his client. She replied that she and the rest of the team had been astounded to learn the identity of 'F', not least because he'd never really been associated with working for the BBC. She elaborated, telling Mr Dunham that she and Meirion had given me their word of honour that they would not reveal his client's identity and that it would be easily applied because their documentary was all about Savile and it wouldn't be necessary to name anyone else. Besides, she said, I'd never claimed Mr Dunham's client had abused me. I'd merely said that when he got close to me and attempted to 'goose' me, I'd reacted badly because he smelled like my stepfather and, in reaction to my reaction, his client had called me a 'titless wonder'.

Mr Dunham spent a considerable period of time trying to persuade Ms MacKean that his client had not, in fact, actually touched me in any way and she was left to try to defend what I'd told her in good faith. Finally, after some thought, she told Mr Dunham that she had believed me when I'd told her that the words 'F' had thoughtlessly hurled at me had been far more memorable and hurtful than the attempted 'goose'. She agreed that, during the seventies, it had been far more acceptable for men of any age to goose a female of any age; it was accepted behaviour and nobody usually complained, or if they did, they were ignored.

When Mr Dunham moved on to how the *Panorama* programme had revealed the identity of his client and asked Ms MacKean why this would be the case, she had to explain, just as Meirion Jones had, that she and the rest of the *Newsnight* team had been completely excluded from the making of the *Panorama* programme. Nobody asked her or, to her knowledge, anyone else, whether there might be any reason not to reveal his client's identity. Mr Dunham wondered aloud whether Ms Ward herself might have given consent and Ms MacKean had no choice but to reply that she didn't know.

The whole morning passed whilst Mr Dunham did his level best to pull Ms MacKean's account to pieces. I didn't know whether he succeeded or not. I felt regret once again that I'd ever breathed a word of any of it. Why hadn't I kept quiet? I could have missed that bit out of my memoir, couldn't I? I knew I couldn't have though, for Savile was the only person who ill-used or abused me in any way whilst I lived at Duncroft. All he'd done was to confirm my firm belief that all men were sex mad and had no respect or liking for a woman at all, seeing her as only a sex slave or unpaid servant doing his housework and bearing his children, often all three at once. In that respect, Savile had probably caused nearly as much damage as those who went before him in relation to me. The Claimant, however, had not abused me physically; he'd just been casually cruel in front of my peer group and a room full of people.

Eventually, that interminable morning came to a close, as did Ms MacKean's cross-examination. I watched her leave the witness stand and then the courtroom and found myself wishing we'd met under better circumstances. I should have liked to be able to call her a friend. At last, the judge dismissed the court and told us to be back at two o'clock; at long last, I could stand and stretch my legs a little.

After a short chat outside the courtroom with David and Helen, Peter and I made our way out into the oppressive London heat, where I began to cough almost immediately. My chest felt tight and, even when I deliberately drew in a huge gulp of air, it didn't feel as if any had actually reached my lungs. My chest felt unpleasantly strange and when I coughed, a sharp pain just beneath my sternum caused me to wince. Peter led me slowly across the busy road and to what had become our accustomed lunch venue and showed concern at the amount of coughing and spluttering I was experiencing.

Somehow, I managed to eat something, and of course, drink tea. Peter said very little during the lunch break, other than to encourage me to use my inhaler and my nitroglycerin pump spray together in order to increase air intake and decrease the chest pain. Of course, as he had known it would, it worked pretty well, but it did cause the mother of all headaches to begin pounding in my temples and the base of my neck…

Chapter Nineteen

Location: inside my own psyche

Timeline: Various

memory: *noun* (plural **memories**): 1. 'The mental capacity or faculty of retaining and reviving facts, events, impressions, etc., or of recalling or recognising previous experiences.'

I'd never really been one who suffered with headaches very much. Other than frequent nosebleeds, generally triggered by catching a clout in the face, my only regular aches were in my lower legs. Nana had always described these dreadful pains, most often suffered at night, as 'growing pains'. One of my own children suffered horribly with the same thing, although he also suffered, and still suffers, regular headaches too. Having said that, there is something about a pain anywhere in the head, be it toothache – which I've suffered a lot – or earache or headache: one cannot escape.

I was pretty adept at being able to dissociate myself from my extremities, mainly because I'd had to learn how to cope with pain on my own. That is, without pain-relieving drugs or other comforts, such as hot water bottles, massage or anything else. Yet, when it came to pain in the head I was far less able to deal with it or find any particular coping method that truly helped. Maybe it was my ability to dissociate from most of my physical body which had allowed me to become so 'resilient' in relation to mental pain and stress. Nevertheless, it would also be true to say that although I coped admirably with virtually all stressful situations, almost always, whilst doing the 'coping' and being 'resilient', my body crept up on me when I wasn't paying attention and did something truly horrible.

Mother suffered a great deal of pain in her neck and head. I had a fleeting memory of her wearing a thick, rubber surgical collar almost constantly when I was around nine or ten... shortly before we moved to Norwich. She had fat ugly scars just above her clavicles, too; there were little scar-dots along the edge of each. When I was very little and she'd been horrible to me, I can recall wondering whether if I managed to 'undo' those scars somehow, maybe whilst she slept, perhaps her vile head might fall off and she'd die...

Perhaps my breathing difficulties were related to being frightened or nervous? Could it be possible to be absolutely scared witless and yet not be aware of that? Memories popped into my mind of myself gasping, unable to get a breath into my lungs at all when confronted with Mother or her foul husband and the impending 'punishment' or other fearful thing – such as water. Hadn't I always had that sensation of my heart feeling as if it were trying to thump its way out of my chest? Yes, I'd felt that for as long as I could recall anything. Surely, if there was anything actually wrong with my heart, they'd have found it, wouldn't they? I mean, I'd had two lots of major surgery and all the tests and whatnot required prior to the actual operations. In fact, it was shortly before the second operation when the hospital had decided I was suffering from COPD. That was weird in itself, because I'd quit smoking just before the first operation in 2011. Weren't you supposed to recover any lost lung function quite quickly when you stopped smoking? I couldn't recall having had any lung problems prior to quitting, but I certainly had them now. Or perhaps it really was, quite simply, 'nerves'.

Nana had often complained of 'nerves' when I was a little child and staying with her, particularly after any unpleasantness between myself and Mother. If I felt sick suddenly, she'd always tell me it was 'probably just nerves' and make a cup of hot chocolate for us both. Actually, that very often worked, although possibly it was Nana's chatter more than the hot, sweet drink. Mother had also complained similarly, although nothing like as passively as Nana. I believe Mother's most well-used phrase was something along the lines of 'Your behaviour is turning me into a nervous wreck'. I was always, without exception, the cause of any illness, upset or anxiety. Even when my little brother caught chicken pox I was held responsible, although the notion was ridiculous since I was barely permitted to be in the same room with him and so catching anything from one another would have been all but impossible.

Being unwell in any way was a crime, as far as Mother was concerned, although only in relation to me. She seemed to deal very well with my little brother whenever he might be poorly with any affliction, whether it be a cold or raging influenza. In fact, the more I thought about it, the more I became convinced that Mother saw me as a sickness, an affliction, undesirable and revolting. Perhaps that might have something to do with my low self-esteem? For it wasn't simply those occasions on which I dared to be unwell which Mother so objected to; she actually had a great deal to say about me in person, healthy or sick. That I was born stupid, or 'retarded' as she liked to put it, was a fact I'd lived with all my life. In fact, any time I did anything innovative or reasonably clever for which Nana or others praised me, Mother would instantly pull me down again with remarks like 'You're not so damned clever, you're as thick as shit, so don't start giving yourself airs or ideas above your station.' Far more personal remarks rained down upon me daily: 'hair like a nest of rat-tails'; 'piggy little eyes'; 'skinny, like a long streak of piss'; and many, many others. In fact, long before the Claimant had ever made his public observations about my lack of womanly curves, Mother had pointed out that my chest was 'as flat as a pancake' and 'you haven't even got an arse round enough to be kicked'.

Looking down at my current ample bust, rolls of flab, pronounced belly and gigantic thighs I wonder why I could never seem to find the happy medium. All my life I'd been stick thin, often looking like the victim of starvation or worse. Always far too fearful that an anaesthetic would cause me to vomit, I'd never been able to pluck up the courage to have surgery to correct what I considered to be my flawed physique. Had I been brave enough, I'd probably have managed to acquire breast implants on the NHS, since my lack caused me such distress, but I'd never even had the courage to approach a doctor and ask.

As I've explained, when I discovered I had cancer of the colon and would need both chemotherapy and surgery, I was more than prepared to die rather than do anything that might cause me to vomit. I made excuses; I pleaded with doctors and surgeons to 'leave me be' but once Peter had explained my precise phobic fear, everything was done to ensure I did not vomit. After the first operation, when I was desperately unwell with infection on top of infection, I remained skeletally thin, but as I recovered, weight had gradually piled on until finally, for the first time in my entire life, I was woman-shaped. Everyone said I looked better for the extra pounds. Personally, I think I now look like my mother, which opens up another Pandora's box entirely.

What might happen after the court case ended and I'd been found guilty, guilty, guilty? Actually, it mattered very little, in my opinion, what might happen to me, for I'd survived everything life had so far chucked in my path and, to the best of my knowledge, one no longer gets thrown into jail for debt. And even if I did, I'd already managed to survive jail once and could do so again.

No, my biggest worry in relation to the case was the fate of other victims, people far less resilient than me. Perhaps they had not yet come forward, or maybe they were thinking about coming forward but, once the newspapers were full of headlines about the woman who had been found guilty of everything possible in relation to calling out perpetrators of abuse or casual cruelty, what then? Back we would all be thrown, into the wells of silence where tears and regrets are muffled beneath the cheers for the great and good – even if in reality they were neither. That may well have been a reasonable and safe place to be prior to 2011, but, due to me and my big mouth, or more accurately, my traitorous fingers, it would be a terrible place to have to return to. It would, surely, have come out anyway? The Savile scandal, I mean. Surely it would have done? Journalists were all over it and I cannot have been the only one to have been hounded and pressured and tricked into speaking out. I actually knew of one alleged victim of Savile who quoted my own memoir, word for word, except she claimed it had been her as the victim and not me. Maybe, if I'd just kept my head down and remained silent, then she could have been the one to cause all the fuss and this blasted case would never have happened at all.

Damn! Damn! Damn! Why can I not shake off the past completely? Am I to be the victim for ever? I don't feel like any kind of victim in myself, but my psyche and my body behave as if they are. Is it normal to keep having flashbacks to things that happened when one was but two or three years old? Do other people freak out in the street when someone walks by wearing a perfume or body odour that reminds them of something bad? Perhaps it's simply the way human beings are built, with these 'big brains' as compared with the smaller brains of other mammals.

Thoughts run away on a tangent for a few moments whilst

I consider the likelihood that other animals suffer from stress, anxiety, flashbacks and terrors and conclude that they most certainly do. So, does that make me more akin to the dog in the shelter that has been thrashed, starved, locked in the dark, kicked about and blamed for things he has no clue about, than to the other ordinary people I meet every day? Again, an affirmative conclusion. Good grief! How on earth have I made it nearly sixty years and how many other people have I, albeit unwittingly, dragged down and damaged with me? There are probably valuable lessons to be learned, but I'm damned if I can figure them out right now, or even face them if I could.

I have a very strong feeling that I'm never going to be permitted to forget this business with Sir Jimmy Savile. As soon as the fuss dies down a bit, somebody comes along and rakes it all up again. For some insane reason, they always seem to come to me first. I wonder why they do that? Do I look like some kind of expert on being abused by an aged nutcase? Evidently, I do, because I always seem to be the person the journalists approach first when they want to know something. Even though I've already told the world everything I know. Perhaps they all think I may have suddenly recalled some juicy piece of smut; after all, I did say that I have, mercifully, forgotten far, far more than I have remembered. Once again, me and my big mouth. I have only myself to blame, then. Just as Mother told me, everything that happened to me was completely and entirely of my own doing. If nothing else, I could create serious grief and total disorder, just by being alive and breathing, she said.

Chapter Twenty

Location: Court 13, Royal Courts of Justice, Strand, London

Timeline: 19 June 2015 – day five of the case

unwilling: *adjective*: 1. 'Not willing; reluctant; loath; averse: *an unwilling partner in the crime*.' 2. 'Opposed; offering resistance; stubborn or obstinate; refractory: *an unwilling captive*.'

I'd been really dreading that afternoon, although I'd not articulated the dread in any verbal way. Although I'd managed, most of the time, to avoid unpleasantness online simply by not seeking out anything or reading anything anybody else found, I was more than aware that Witness 'C' was absolutely livid at having been drawn into the case. Actually, Helen had told me Witness 'C' had taken great exception to something I'd written in my memoir and so was enraged about that as well.

My heart hammered hard against my ribs when Witness 'C' was called to the witness box, but the woman who entered the court and wearily took the stand was as unfamiliar to me as a total stranger. The passage of more than forty years had hardly changed Susan Bunce at all, I thought. How on earth could it have ravaged this poor woman so? I leaned in towards Helen and whispered, 'Did we absolutely have to do this?' She replied, 'Yes, we absolutely did have to.'

Once she began to answer Mr Dunham's questions, I realised that the voice of Witness 'C' had not changed a jot. I closed my eyes and, as she spoke, could see in my mind's eye the bubbly blonde-haired girl with the merry, mischievous eyes once more. We hadn't exactly been friends, but generally Witness 'C' had been a pleasant person who muddled along pretty well with just about everyone, including me.

Mr Dunham was making some kind of reference to the fact that he believed Witness 'C' had not, in fact, been at the television theatre on the same evening as I had. Of course, she insisted she had been, otherwise how could she have met his client and been so utterly offended by him? There followed two or three instances of laptops and memory sticks being passed around, one to the judge, of course, and the others to Witness 'C' and to me and my team. Mr Dunham was endeavouring to ascertain if certain young women on the film excerpts of the show were Witness 'C'. She dismissed them all; none of them was her.

There followed questions about who had attended the theatre on the evening in question and Witness 'C' replied, in an uninterested tone, that Susan and Keri (the name by which I had been known from childhood, even though, as I have said, it was not on my birth certificate) had been there but she couldn't recall who else. Mr Dunham tried very hard indeed to get her to tell the court what she'd been wearing, how she had travelled to London, how long the visit had taken and what had occurred. To all of these questions she replied, 'Dunno, can't remember.' I'm fairly certain that Mr Dunham had planned to try to persuade Witness 'C' that her memory was faulty but he didn't have to try very hard at all, and when he suggested her memory was almost non-existent, she agreed that it probably was. I tried not to let my smirk of satisfaction be seen, because Mr Dunham was clearly temporarily surprised. Evidently, he hadn't expected Witness 'C' to be quite so easy to pull to pieces.

In back of the court I was aware that Susan Bunce sat alongside her friend known online as Anna Raccoon. That lady had travelled all the way from France to be in court. She was one of those who denied everything that had been uncovered about Jimmy Savile and she had, in fact, written quite a lot of extremely unpleasant and detrimental stuff about me in her blog, denouncing me as a liar and troublemaker along with other less-savoury titles. I'd never met the woman, and although I avoided reading anything about myself, Helen had found several pieces to which she had drawn my attention. I'd been surprised by the vitriolic nature of the woman's feelings towards me. How on earth could she so detest someone she'd never met? I wondered. Not far away from those two sat a trio of women, all more or less in my age bracket. I wondered who they were. They didn't interact with Susan or 'Ms Raccoon' but when I turned and glanced at them, all three shot daggers at me. I quickly turned to face front.

The questions continued and Witness 'C' continued to answer most of them with the phrase 'Can't remember.'

Eventually, Mr Dunham received an answer of more than those two words. Witness 'C' described the room we had been gathered in after the show had been filmed in a similar way to me, although she recalled even less detail. When asked about the interaction between me and the Claimant, Witness 'C' had replied, in a dismissive tone, that Keri had become hysterical about something the Claimant said or did, but that she'd no memory of hearing or seeing anything at all. When he challenged Witness 'C' that nothing at all had happened between his client and herself on that evening, she replied, 'Oh, yes, it did. I remember that bit well.'

I listened to the exchange between Mr Dunham and Witness 'C' with only half an ear because, once again, my attention had drifted. I could not recall anything of what had happened to Witness 'C' that evening. I pondered the fact of my self-centredness; were all adolescent girls as inward-looking as me? Obviously not, for Susan had recalled a great deal which didn't directly involve her.

Witness 'C' described how she had been enjoying herself that evening and had approached the Claimant to speak with him. During the course of the conversation, she'd asked if she could have a memento, something to remind her of the evening and the meeting. The Claimant had laughingly replied with a question, asking whether she would like a lock of his hair. She had agreed, immediately, that she would and then been dismayed as he thrust his hand down the front of his trousers and produced a couple of hairs, adding the words, 'pubic hair, I mean'. She'd been understandably upset and disgusted, more so when Jimmy Savile, who was standing nearby, had added that pubic hair was a good present to offer because 'they like to give head'. Why I had forgotten this I cannot say. Actually, even hearing Witness 'C' relate it to the court, I still had little in the way of recall, only of some general laughter and a bit of shouting on the way back to Duncroft in the minibus.

It was just after she'd told the court what the Claimant had said and done that Witness 'C' suddenly glanced across the courtroom and caught my eye. Her expression showed pure hatred of me. She'd been unwilling to get involved with the case; she'd not even made any statement about Savile so keen was she to remain anonymous, although she had spoken, briefly, by private message to Liz MacKean on the site Friends Reunited. Now, not only had I and my legal team forced her against her better judgement and free will to take part in the court proceedings, but she'd had to relive the event in open court. I didn't blame her one bit. I'd have given anything, absolutely anything, for all the business about Savile and the Claimant and all the other famous people being revealed as abusers not to have happened, much less to have drawn me (or Witness 'C') into the limelight, all unwilling and for the whole country to pass judgement upon.

At one point, I recall the judge himself asking Witness 'C' something, but I was too miserable in my own self-pity to take much notice. Briefly, I wondered what the inhabitants of the country would be thinking about me and other girls from Duncroft. Fortunately, I managed to shake off that particular shackle very quickly; I've always tried hard to disregard what everyone thinks, with the exception of those I love, whose opinions matter deeply to me. Although I managed to shake free the cloying feelings of being judged by the general public, not to mention Witness 'C' herself, I couldn't, however, resolve the guilt I felt in having brought Witness 'C' to court in the first place. No wonder she hated me now; in her shoes, I'd feel just the same.

Mr Dunham tried several different tactics to try to make holes in Witness 'C''s account but he was unsuccessful. Although she'd said as little as possible, she was adamant about what she did articulate and there was no shaking her, even though she readily agreed that her general memories of Duncroft, other residents, outings and so forth were almost nil.

The afternoon seemed to drag interminably. How could time pass so very slowly? I wondered, more than once. Doubtless, poor Witness 'C' was feeling likewise. She sounded tired, bored and uninterested. When, at long last, her cross-examination ended, she left the witness box without looking around the court at all. I turned to watch her leave and noticed that the three women left the court too. Perhaps they'd been friends or relatives of Witness 'C'. Whoever they were, they evidently didn't like me because they all glared at me as they left.

I hoped that the court would be adjourned for the day, but David began to address the judge and some legal argument commenced. Helen whispered to me that this was perfectly normal and I shouldn't be alarmed. I listened without much interest, as most of what was being discussed was way beyond my comprehension. I knew nothing about torts or other, similar cases or pleadings.

Finally, after about a decade, the judge informed the court that he intended to 'set judgment aside' and that legal arguments and other matters would bring the case to a close the following day. Whilst I was still wondering what that actually meant, the clerk called, 'All rise.'

David wore an expression of great satisfaction and lost no time in telling me he had been very pleased with the evidence Witness 'C' had given, even though she'd been unwilling to take any part in the case. I asked if he could be certain that her identity would remain secret or whether the reporters might let slip who she really was. He chuckled and remarked that no reporter would dare reveal the lady's identity after having been told by a High Court judge not to do so. Not unless he or she fancied a spell of imprisonment for contempt of court.

As we left the building alongside David and Helen, I asked what the judge had meant when he'd said he intended to set judgment aside and David explained that it merely meant the judge would, when the case concluded, take the documentation and everything he'd personally noted and study the case at his leisure in some great detail before making any judgment. At first I was horrified, and asked if that meant Peter and I would be required to remain in London indefinitely until judgment had been made. David explained that would not be necessary and I breathed an undisguised sigh of relief and told him that Peter and I were very nearly out of resources with which to remain in the city. Peter had used all his credit cards and both of us had cleared out our bank accounts to pay for fares, food, hotels and so forth. To my surprise, David then told us we had no need to remain in London any longer or even to attend court any further because the legal argument would be prolonged and we would, no doubt, find it dreadfully dreary.

'Do you mean we are free to return home?' I asked, incredulous. David said we were and that he would keep in touch and let us know as soon as he heard anything of interest. He thanked me for doing everything he'd asked of me and then turned to thank Peter for his support of me. With hardly any more said, Helen and David headed back to their office and Peter and I were left on the pavement outside the Royal Courts of Justice, stunned by our sudden freedom.

Chapter Twenty-One

Location: at home in Shropshire

Timeline: 20 June–9 July 2015

home: *noun*: 1. 'A house, apartment, or other shelter that is the usual residence of a person, family, or household.' 2. 'The place in which one's domestic affections are centred.'

I'd been so desperate to get home, partly because I think, deep down, I'd felt when I left to go to London for the court case that I'd not be coming back – I'd have been flung in jail or something (even though I was fully aware that this no longer happened). Arriving home felt incredibly special to me. All three sons were there at one time or another during the day, each full of hugs and reassurance. My two daft dogs, Oakley and Willow, were as thrilled to see me as if I'd been absent for years; the cats were less enthusiastic, but after a cool greeting, one after another demanded attention and affection. Peter had been even more eager to get home to his house because his collie-cross bitch, pregnant by my collie-cross dog, had given birth on the second night we were away. Sadly, the vet had to be summoned to assist and the first puppy, a large female, had been born dead. The second pup, equally large and male, had survived. Peter's family had been sending emails and text photographs of Cedar (the bitch) and the little fellow most evenings and we'd both seen how much the youngster grew in just a few days.

I settled immediately into my old familiar lifestyle, which involved about as much excitement and variety as usual – that is to say, zero. I revelled in the slow pace of life in the sleepy little village after the frenetic pace of London and gratefully sucked in huge lungfuls of the clean, fresh air (well, aside from the odd bit of muck-spreading) as I accompanied my two doggies, albeit extremely slowly and with much huffing and puffing, up the hill of the local nature reserve, land reclaimed from the spoil of the old coal mine. At the summit, where a commemorative mosaic was made a few years ago by local groups and businesses, the view is stupendous. On a bright, sunny day, one can see for miles in all directions. Closer to, trees in their full summer foliage, leaves whispering arboreal secrets to one another in the faint breeze, grow scattered on the slopes and throughout the distant landscapes below and around. I felt astonished, in some strange way, to be standing there, observing nature in all its glory, even if Oakley was doing his utmost to uproot a sapling and Willow busy digging for some imaginary treasure on the hilltop. I encountered a few of my dog-walker friends and their furry charges and answered their concerned questions about the case and the Claimant. Everyone was incredibly supportive and I felt very lucky indeed to have such a lovely area and such great people to return home to.

I went over to Peter's home a couple of days after we returned because I wanted to see the new puppy, Bramble. Cedar greeted me as enthusiastically as my own dogs and proudly showed me her offspring, who was quite possibly the largest week-old puppy I'd ever seen in my entire life. I sat there in the sitting room of Peter's home and spoke with both his dad and his disabled mum about the puppy, the case and how London had been, and of how very glad I felt to be safely home again. Of course, they asked when we'd know the outcome and both Peter and I had to admit we had no idea. Jacqui, Peter's mum, remarked that she thought I'd have nothing at all to worry about if I'd told the truth. I told her I most sincerely hoped that was true.

The following day, Peter visited me in the late afternoon and told me his mum had been admitted to hospital. Immediately concerned, I asked what the problem might be as she'd seemed well enough when we spoke, and he said she had a chest infection which came on suddenly and that the hospital had also diagnosed heart failure. I must have looked appalled because he quickly added that heart failure isn't actually as dreadful as it sounds in all cases. He felt quite certain there was little to be concerned about and, since he is a qualified nurse well used to caring for both elderly and disabled patients, I had no reason to question his opinion.

Over the following few days, both Peter and I spent some considerable time with the dogs. He brought Cedar and the puppy over to my home so that Oakley and Willow could meet Bramble and get to know him as Cedar's youngster.

Everything went well and little Bramble was accepted into our doggy pack immediately. London and the court case seemed like a lifetime ago and I tried my best to put the whole thing out of my mind entirely. Of course, now and then, people asked me how things had gone or, for some unknown reason, a moment from the proceedings or something one of the witnesses had said crossed my mind, but I refused to dwell on it during the day.

Unfortunately, at night, once Peter had gone home, thoughts of the case and of the impending judgment, certain to be a final, personal disaster for me, kept me from sleeping. I had trouble getting to sleep and then trouble staying asleep. Strangely, though, waking up after I'd finally passed out from sheer exhaustion was just as difficult and I felt neither refreshed nor rested. Dark circles began to appear beneath my eyes and I yawned frequently throughout the day, every day. Somehow, if Peter was visiting, I could fall asleep on the settee at the drop of a hat and, bless him, he always let me sleep and never once crept off and left me alone. Even though I never actually told Peter how much the pending result of the case played on my mind, I'm perfectly certain he knew full well. He always seemed to be there just exactly where and when he was needed.

I had an appointment with my psychologist, Dr Isabel Goodwin, on Monday 29 June. It was such a relief to finally be able to unburden all my anxieties, worries, stupid preconceptions and barely suppressed panic. I spent a very beneficial two hours with the psychologist who, in her gently calm and expert manner, helped me to sort the wheat from the chaff, as it were. We managed to shelve preposterous anxieties and totally unreasonable fears where they should be: under 'junk'. With Dr Goodwin's help, I realised what my real deep-down concerns were, whether they were well founded or if I'd expanded them, mentally, out of proportion. We also discussed the possible outcomes of the case and, of course, the implications of the judge finding me guilty of libel, slander and defamation.

During that meeting I discovered that I was far more altruistic than I'd ever believed myself to be; I'd always considered myself to be a fundamentally selfish person. Mother had drummed it into my head that I was as self-centred as a gyroscope all my life, until I finally escaped her clutches by accepting a bribe of a couple of hundred pounds to 'Go away and never, ever come back.' However, Dr Goodwin made me realise that my worries actually centred upon other victims, particularly those who had not yet come forward, or who never would come forward if the case went against me. It was quite a shock to discover that I'd actually completely given up hope for myself and that I neither worried nor cared what might happen to me. I had nothing to lose. I'd never had any money or any grand possessions, so I'd never, ever have any hope of paying up three hundred thousand pounds in compensation, never mind the costs. All that bothered me was, once again, that I'd not be believed and others would suffer because of that. I felt considerably better when I left the community mental-health building that afternoon, though, and I slept a little better that night, too.

Shortly before the court case, I'd been invited down to London to the premiere of a play about Jimmy Savile written by Jonathan Maitland. As I was getting ready for the evening performance, Peter noticed one side of my face had 'fallen' slightly compared to the other. I did feel a bit 'queer', but thought it was probably nerves because I knew I'd be obliged to speak to the press about the play. Peter was very worried because he thought I'd had a mini-stroke or a TIA (transient ischaemic attack, or mini-stroke) but I dismissed his worries out of hand, saying I didn't have time for such things and the sooner we got the blasted play viewed and the interviews over, the sooner we could go home.

A few days later, I went to see the GP who, on listening to the account of the event, sent me straight to hospital. This happened on Friday 12 June and the hospital consultant tried to have me admitted for tests. I flatly refused because, I explained to him, I needed to be in court on 15 June. The doctor retorted that the court would have to wait and I argued that one didn't expect a High Court to 'wait' for anything. On the promise that I would attend an outpatient appointment after the case, he reluctantly allowed me to discharge myself. That outpatient appointment was on 3 July and, our part in the court case over, Peter accompanied me, teasing and laughing because it turned out be in the Department for Elderly Medicine, at which I pretended to be offended. Fortunately, the consultant there decided, after many questions and a close study of my enormous medical file, that I probably hadn't suffered a stroke after all. Relieved, we left and I had just asked Peter to please drive me home via

Sainsbury's and the vet's when the consultant called me and asked me to return urgently to his clinic.

Panic-stricken, we hurried back to the hospital and whilst Peter searched for a parking space, I raced back into the clinic, my eyes wide with undisguised terror. Mr Khan invited me straight back into his office and explained, before Peter arrived, that he'd noticed some recent test results in my notes which showed I had a severe problem with my liver. He bombarded me with questions, in particular wanting to know how much alcohol I drank. He didn't appear to be convinced when I replied that I never touch alcohol, even when Peter arrived and confirmed this to be the case. He sent me down to phlebotomy to have a series of blood samples taken to check for hepatitis in all its forms, along with several other tests, including HIV.

A feeling of deep gloom settled on me as Peter drove me home; I found it quite difficult to concentrate on what I needed from the supermarket and found myself staring stupidly at items on shelves, not knowing whether they were even familiar, never mind whether I needed them or not. Beside me, Peter was a reassuring presence even though he didn't say much. I'm sure, though, he was probably thinking hard about what the problem could possibly be. By the time we got to the checkouts, my brain was even more addled than usual and without thinking I answered my mobile when it rang, not even glancing to see who the caller might be.

The shopping bag fell from my fingers as I recognised Helen's voice. She said, simply, 'OK to talk?' I believe I replied along the lines of 'Uh-huh'. Peter stopped packing and watched my face intently. With no further ado, Helen said, 'Kat, you won.'

In a split second I wondered whether to let my knees go limp and fold me gently to the floor, whether to vomit, whether to whoop with triumph or burst into tears. I actually did none of those things. I said, 'Beg pardon?' To which Helen repeated herself and added that I absolutely must not tell anybody at all until the verdict was handed down in court, which was scheduled for Friday, 10 July. Apparently, if I told a soul, I'd be in contempt of court and risk imprisonment or an enormous fine. David joined in the conversation by some mechanism I fail to understand and congratulated me warmly. He asked me how it felt to be believed by someone as important as a High Court judge, but I couldn't think of an answer at the time. I told him something, he congratulated me again and the call ended. I looked up. Peter had paid for the shopping on my behalf and packed it, too. He steered me and the trolley containing the bags out to the car park and said not one word until we were in the car.

He said I'd won the case and I couldn't hide the broad smile that had affixed itself to my cheeks, which ached in protest because I rarely smile, certainly not for any prolonged period. I replied that I couldn't say because I was absolutely not allowed to tell a soul or I'd be held in contempt of court. He remarked that I didn't need to tell him; he'd watched about a hundredweight of care lift away from me in front of his eyes. As he drove towards the vet's, I explained that we'd need to be in London for ten in the morning on 10 July to hear the verdict handed down. With his usual calm aplomb, he assured me he would arrange further time off work in order to drive me there and back.

As we left the veterinary building clutching a bag of medicines for my sick cat, we bumped into Peter's sister Mandy accompanied by his dad, Andy. Apparently, Mandy's cat had been neutered and they'd come to collect him. However, Andy was feeling very angry and frustrated because he'd been to the hospital in Shrewsbury to collect his wife who had been declared fit enough to return home and yet, after waiting for nearly two hours, had to leave because there had been a problem with her medication and, as an insulin-dependent diabetic, she could not leave without the stuff. He was to return at five to try to collect her again. Peter and his dad were deep in conversation and I knew Peter was explaining what the hospital could and couldn't do with Jacqui's possessions and prescription medicines. I left them and went to the car because, in truth, my legs suddenly felt weak and more than anything, I needed to sit down. I couldn't wait to get home and really relax with a cup of tea.

Much later that evening, I sat in the lounge at Peter's home and listened as Jacqui described her stay in the hospital and how one elderly and confused lady had been convinced Jacqui was her long-lost daughter. We chatted and laughed over the puppy's antics and at the way Mandy's cat was still enraged at having been abandoned at the vet and so was making everyone pay for it with angry glares and grumbles. Shortly before I left to return home, Jacqui asked me, full of concern, 'Peter tells me you're not very well yourself. Something about your liver?' I assured her I was certain the hospital had made some kind of error because I felt fine, better than I'd done in years in fact, and told her to concentrate on clearing her infection and not to worry about me and 'mythical liver problems'. She laughed and I said goodnight. Since Peter had work from the next day, which was Sunday, through till Thursday, I'd not be seeing him until early Friday morning when we'd leave for London and the court.

I spent Sunday with two of my three sons and did very little other than catch up on a little laundry whilst promising myself I'd get to work writing the very next morning. I watched television until late, read even later and then went off to sleep as easily as could be. I awoke the next morning feeling rested for the first time I could recall in years. After a leisurely breakfast I was sitting at the computer about to open a new Word document when my mobile rang. I glanced down and saw it was Peter calling. I answered with a cheery, 'Hiya, you not at work?' His reply caused my hair to stand on end and my breath to catch in my throat.

'Mum just died.'

Chapter Twenty-Two

**Location: Court 13, Royal Courts of Justice,
Queen's Bench Division, Strand, London**

Timeline: 10 July 2015

justice: *noun*: 'Fairness in the way people are dealt with.'

Despite leaving Shropshire at the ridiculously early hour of five in the morning, Peter and I actually arrived in court after the judge had entered and started handing down his judgment. If there had been *any* way that I could have avoided being present in court that morning, I'd have taken it but, in view of the fact that the judge had found in my favour and with the anticipated 'media-storm' that would trigger, both Helen and David told me I really had to be there.

To my surprise, the Claimant himself was not in court, and Mr Dunham remained devoid of facial expression as the judge continued reading out his judgment. I glanced at David and saw his barely suppressed delight even though his expression was respectfully serious. I'd received a draft copy of the judgment from Helen by email and had read it through very carefully, noting that the judge deemed me partly responsible for the airing of the ITV words 'I was horribly, horribly humiliated by [the Claimant]' as a 'co-publisher'. It turned out not to matter anyway, because the judge had decided that my words were true and therefore I had not slandered, libelled or defamed the Claimant.

When David and Mr Dunham stood to discuss the costs of the case and by what date the Claimant would be required to pay them, Helen leaned close to me and whispered something about the Claimant wishing he'd never begun this. I agreed, somewhat vacantly. I jolly well wished he'd never started this. Only at that point did the anger rise within me. Had the Claimant actually been in court that morning, there is an extremely strong possibility I may well have surged to my feet and launched a tirade at him. He'd made such an enormous mountain out of little more than a molehill; if he had received the news of what I'd said about him with less panic and hysteria, none of this need have occurred. A great deal of money could have been saved, an awful lot of grief and pain avoided and court time allocated to something more deserving.

Most importantly to me, Peter would not be sitting beside me in a courtroom when his mum had died only four days previously and he was badly needed at home. That was probably the one thing I could not accept or get past. I'd become so used to trouble, grief, pain, harassment and all the other negative crap life had flung at me for the best part of fifty-seven-and-a-quarter years, and this was the real reason for my so-called 'resilience' to it all. That Peter, who had never asked for or deserved such appalling pressure on his psyche, his heart and his wallet – being guilty only of caring and trying to protect me from the mud constantly thrown in my face – could not remain at home to mourn his mother's passing was the one thing I could never, ever forgive the Claimant for.

I screamed my regrets silently, unable even to find simple words to express my gratitude to this self-effacing man who had stuck by me through thick and thin, never asking anything of me and expecting nothing in return. It dawned on me, as I sat there, wishing all manner of impossible things whilst Peter sat beside me, ever dependable, that I trusted him. That is no meaningless thing for one as damaged in the ways I've been damaged. In fact, it is astounding and, I would have said, prior to that realisation, impossible, for I had never been able to trust anyone completely (furry people don't count).

I had met Peter in early 2002 via his sister, with whom I was friendly. Although he had problems of his own, for some reason, we began a relationship and merged our two families together (he was also a single parent). This was a disaster. His kids hated mine and vice versa, and resentment and many other negatives served to quickly destroy any actual relationship. We separated but remained friends. Peter trained as a nurse and, when I was diagnosed with cancer, was my rock and total support. After chemoradiotherapy and an almost fatal surgery and multiple infections, through which Peter nursed me, when the local council awarded me care in the community, because he lives more than ten miles away, I was able to employ him as my personal nurse/PA. However, I am awarded thirty hours' care a week and Peter puts in many, many more hours than I can pay him for. We are very close friends and happy to live twelve miles apart rather than be in any form of relationship.

Suddenly, the court was standing and the judge retired. Smiles all round; even the few reporters in court were smiling. Helen confided that she was absolutely terrified of being required to make a statement on my behalf and I told her she was frightfully intimidating and would come across very well. I hadn't actually intended to say anything at all myself. I'd collaborated with Helen via email over the previous day or two, to construct a statement for the press, and we had agreed she would read it out to any media people wanting such a thing.

Even though I had expected there to be interest in the case, I really was not at all prepared for what met us as we descended the steps of the Royal Courts of Justice: television camera crews, reporters waving notebooks and microphones, and photographers darting this way and that constantly snapping pictures. It was a veritable melee and for two pins I'd have turned and fled back into the cool gloom of the court building. Peter squeezed my fingers and then stepped aside in order that the photographers and cameramen could focus just on me. Several of those gathered urged me to speak, to say something, make a comment and, in spite of what Helen and I had agreed, I did speak.

I said that it (the whole court case) should never have happened. What I'd meant was that it should never have been allowed to have happened. I tried to speak to other victims and reassure them that it would be safe to come forward. I think, actually, my words were garbled and certainly, in the few photographs I couldn't miss seeing in the following days, my facial expression was stern – at least I didn't look as intimidated by it all as I felt.

Helen, an enormous presence in spite of her diminutive stature, stood and read out her speech. I couldn't help thinking, as she read from the prepared statement, that she had a most wonderful voice that would have been perfect for radio! Finally, the crowd parted and we could make our way onto Fleet Street and along towards David's office.

Congratulations, thanks and farewells didn't take very long and, before an hour had passed, we were headed towards the motorway to return home. However, Jonathan Maitland, bless him, had introduced me to one Jonathan Hartley, a publicity and media agent, and he'd managed to arrange, in short order, for me to do an exclusive interview with a reporter from the *Mail on Sunday*. Peter obligingly turned around and we met the reporter on the concourse of St Pancras station. The interview took an hour or more and then we were free to return home. Stopping only to purchase sandwiches and drinks, Peter headed into the traffic on the M1 motorway, which was jam-packed and at a total standstill. It was one of the hottest days of the year so far and the sun burned relentlessly down as we sat in traffic barely moving. It took nearly nine hours to get back to Shropshire.

In theory, that should have been that. It should have all been over and done with, right? Wrong. The Claimant, Freddie Starr, had liquidated all his assets and left the country. He'd bought himself a modest apartment in Spain and did not pay the costs as ordered by the High Court. He'd actually done this just a few days into the actual trial! No wonder he hadn't been in court. Had he known, I wondered, that he would not win the case he'd brought against me? Surely, that was impossible. I hadn't known I'd win; in fact, I'd been certain I'd lose and be ruined.

David Price had acted for me on a conditional fee arrangement (CFA), which meant, basically, 'no win, no fee' and, since I'd won, I had nothing to pay. However, David and Helen, Yinka and Stuart had all worked so very hard on my behalf and had not been paid. The bill was enormous, of course. I think it was somewhere in the region of half a million pounds, although some newspapers placed it at closer to a million. Freddie Starr had brought this action against me whilst having no thought that he might be required to pay anything. Rumours had it that his brief, Mr Dunham, had acted for him free of charge, but as I said, that is simply a rumour and Mr Dunham isn't about to make any public statement on the matter.

At the time of writing, I've been obliged to sign further CFA's in order for David Price to endeavour to recoup some of his losses by pursuing Freddie Starr in the Spanish courts. In fact, Freddie Starr still insists what I've said is not true; that lovely lady reporter who interviewed me has also been to interview him at his new apartment in Spain and he repeated this to her. According to Mr Starr, he has no money and is unable to settle the legal bill even in part, or so he told the reporter.

I continue to be called on by various reporters, biographers, documentary-makers and others for my opinions, feelings and thoughts about one Sir Jimmy Savile, OBE, and not one of them seems to be capable of understanding that I no longer feel or think anything at all about him. Or of the past, or Duncroft, or anything else from my miserable life. Now, I simply take one day at a time and hope to goodness I can finally write something worthwhile and readable from which I may, one day, either make a living of sorts or leave something for my boys. There is a great deal of 'past' to ignore and, I hope, at least some 'future' to look forward to.

*

'You may choose to look the other way
but you can never again say that you did not know'
William Wilberforce (1759–1833)